McGRAW-HILL

INDUSTRIAL ORGANIZATION AND MANAGEMENT SERIES

L. C. Morrow, *Consulting Editor*

★ ★ ★

Constructive Collective Bargaining

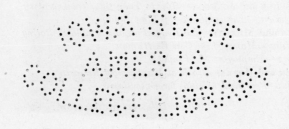

*The quality of the materials used in
the manufacture of this book is governed by continued postwar shortages.*

McGRAW-HILL

INDUSTRIAL ORGANIZATION AND MANAGEMENT SERIES

L. C. MORROW, *Consulting Editor*
Editor, Factory Management and Maintenance

Assisted by a Board of Industrial and Educational Advisers

(*Books already published or in production*)

BENSON—*Music and Sound Systems in Industry*

BETHEL, ATWATER, SMITH and STACKMAN—*Industrial Organization and Management*

BIKLEN and BRETH—*The Successful Employee Publication*

BRIDGES—*Job Placement of the Physically Handicapped*

CANTOR—*Employee Counseling*

CHEYFITZ—*Constructive Collective Bargaining*

DICKIE—*Production With Safety*

ELLS—*Salary and Wage Administration*

EVANS—*A Program for Personnel Administration*

FERN—*Training for Supervision in Industry*

FITZPATRICK—*Understanding Labor*

GARDINER—*When Foreman and Steward Bargain*

GILBRETH and COOK—*The Foreman in Manpower Management*

GRANT—*Statistical Quality Control*

HANNAFORD—*Conference Leadership in Business and Industry*

HILL and HOOK—*Management at the Bargaining Table*

HYDE—*Fundamentals of Successful Manufacturing*

KALSEM—*Practical Supervision*

LINCOLN—*Lincoln's Incentive System*

LIPPERT—*Accident Prevention Administration*

MORGAN—*Industrial Training and Testing*

NEUSCHEL and JOHNSON—*How to Take Physical Inventory*

PRESGRAVE—*The Dynamics of Time Study*

SMYTH and MURPHY—*Job Evaluation and Employee Rating*

STOWERS—*Management Can Be Human*

TOOTLE—*Employees Are People*

WIREN and HEYEL—*Practical Management Research*

YOUNG—*Personnel Manual for Executives*

(*Other titles in preparation*)

Constructive
Collective Bargaining

BY

EDWARD T. CHEYFITZ

*Assistant to Eric A. Johnston, President Motion
Picture Association of America, Inc.*

First Edition

New York   *London*

McGRAW-HILL BOOK COMPANY, INC.

1947

THE MAPLE PRESS COMPANY, YORK, PA.

PREFACE

There is no easy road to industrial peace.

This truism has not, however, permeated America's present thinking on industrial relations. Too many people still believe that industrial peace can be obtained by passing a law. They cling to the illusion that we can legislate ourselves into a Shangri-La of industrial harmony.

We are going to get new labor legislation in 1947. And some is necessary. But most of what we get will be bad—will hurt rather than help employer-employee relations. For pending legislation, reflecting popular opinion, flows from two current myths:

1. That society cannot depend upon voluntary collective bargaining for industrial peace.

2. That legislation and a strong government can compel industrial peace.

Too many people have written off the institution of collective bargaining. For them, collective bargaining has failed. They feel it must be abandoned or drastically modified before economic chaos destroys us completely.

The public thinking which now accepts the breakdown of collective bargaining as complete and final can be charged to the wave of strikes that have occurred since the war's end. Emotional reactions to unprecedented national strikes in our basic industries have clouded reason and perspective. This feeling of pessimism and despair is somewhat reminiscent of the panicky jackal in the old Hindu verse.

> *In April was the jackal born,*
> *In June the rain-fed rivers swelled:*
> *"Never in all my life," said he,*
> *"Have I so great a flood beheld."*

v

Our "April to June" thinking on labor relations has led us to the hasty conclusion that collective bargaining as the principal means for obtaining industrial peace must now be abandoned. And this in spite of the fact that collective bargaining in our mass-production industries has not yet genuinely been tried. What are really the birth pains of collective bargaining are being misinterpreted widely as its death pains. And so the notion is prevalent that we must seek new means to eliminate strikes and achieve harmonious employer-employee relations.

But with all the searching and seeking for new means we must eventually face the reality that the alternative to collective bargaining, no matter how sugar-coated, is government compulsion. And that is no alternative in a free society.

The arguments against compulsion are well known. It is difficult for government to fix wages through compulsory arbitration without regulating every segment of our economy. It is impossible to eliminate strikes without creating a police state. There is the additional argument—Will compulsion work?

The idea that strikes can be eliminated by passing a law is about as practical as prohibiting divorce to achieve happy marriages. As has often been pointed out, Australia and New Zealand have compulsory arbitration but they have never eliminated strikes. They have succeeded only in promoting illegal strikes.

Does the abhorrence of compulsion mean that government has no role to play in industrial relations? Quite the contrary. Government has much to do. It should provide a neutral, competent mediation service to facilitate agreement-making where necessary. It should encourage voluntary arbitration by providing inexpensive arbitration services. It should help eliminate abuses that undermine collective bargaining. It should set up "rules of the game" that encourage labor and management to resolve their differences. All this and more government can and should do. But all that government does must hinge on the premise that *in a free society there is no alternative to voluntary collective bargaining.*

The development of collective bargaining as an effective technique for eliminating work stoppages is not enough. Collective bargaining must also be dedicated to the objectives of economic progress—high-level employment, production, and consumption. To adapt the collective bargaining technique to these needs—industrial peace and economic progress—is the job ahead. That means we ought to be applying American initiative and ingenuity toward making collective bargaining work instead of seeking illusory panaceas in our legislative halls.

America continues to devote so much talk and energy to the issue of whether or not collective bargaining should be established that only meager attention has been devoted to *the development of collective bargaining itself.* George W. Taylor, who as national chairman of the War Labor Board was intimately acquainted with hundreds of management-union relationships, sums it up this way:

> Despite the crucial functions which have been assigned to collective bargaining, there has been relatively little thought and effort given to the constructive development of the collective bargaining process.

And that is the excuse for this book—the hope of contributing to "the constructive development of the collective bargaining process," for without constructive collective bargaining there can be no strong, united, free America.

EDWARD T. CHEYFITZ.

WASHINGTON, D.C.,
March, 1947.

CONTENTS

	PAGE
PREFACE	V
CHAPTER	
I. LIVING TOGETHER	1
II. LET FREEDOM RING!	10
III. THREE MAGIC LETTERS: PMH	20
IV. LEGISLATIVE-EXECUTIVE-JUDICIAL	32
V. FROM COLLECTIVE BARGAINING TO COOPERATIVE PLANNING	45
VI. HOW FAST IS FAST?	55
VII. PRIVATE ENTERPRISE ON THE JOB!	69
VIII. WHAT'S A MAN WORTH?	79
IX. WHY DOESN'T THE GOVERNMENT DO SOMETHING?	89
X. DON'T WORK YOURSELF OUT OF A JOB!	101
XI. STRAWS IN THE WIND	111
XII. CONCLUSION	119
Appendix A. EYE TO EYE	125
Appendix B. CHARTER OF THE TOLEDO LABOR-MANAGEMENT-CITIZENS COMMITTEE	150
INDEX	157

CHAPTER I

LIVING TOGETHER

A man digs a ditch.

A boy asks the man, "Why do you dig the ditch?"

"To earn money," he answers.

"Why do you need money?" the boy presses.

The man replies, "To buy food—to keep my strength."

"And why do you need strength?"

"To dig a ditch."

We work so that we may eat, so that we may live, so that we may work. For much of mankind, for thousands of years, this has been life's cycle, too often a vicious one. But always as man worked, he planned and dreamed of ways to lighten this constant burden of getting food and shelter.

Man's struggle for existence led him to the discovery of tools. He learned to implement his own strength and energy. The use of tools in turn led him to another discovery. He soon found that by combining his mental, physical, and tool resources with those of other men, he could accomplish things that were otherwise impossible. He learned that *group living was the most effective way to survive.* Society was born.

Since man first came on earth he has been constantly seeking the answer to how men can most efficiently organize themselves to obtain the material things necessary to life. The problem of effective economic organization has varied with man's technical development. Until recently the problem has been primarily one of *how* relatively scarce resources, both human and natural, could be utilized so that the greatest possible amount of material goods and services would result. Today science has made many former scarce resources abundant. We have won our

1

struggle with our environment. Nature, once the enemy, has become the friend. We have learned the secret of obtaining material abundance. Now, we need only to learn to live together.

Through the years man has not sought bread alone. Words such as "liberty," "freedom," "individuality," "human dignity," and "human rights" have come to mean as much as food, shelter, and clothing. Man is physically, psychologically, and spiritually constituted as an individual. He constantly strives for the right of self-expression. Man thus finds himself in this dilemma: In the struggle for survival, man must work with his fellow men. Man strives for more and more material goods of life through group living. At the same time he seeks to safeguard and expand his individual freedom. The harmonizing of these two forces, group living and individual liberties, underlies a successful solution of the problem of effective social organization in any age. "Living together" must embrace the concept of individual freedom.

In the search for effective group living man has clung to a fundamental approach. We call it democracy. But democracy itself is not an objective. It is a means to an end. Democracy has been called a way of life. It is exactly that. It is a manner of living—group living. It is a vehicle, an instrumentality, a mechanism that we apply to group living in order that we may achieve our objectives of *material* and *mental* well-being. Because democracy permits individual expression, it is the only manner of living that will give us freedom as well as security. The sum total of individual expressions guarantees that the group will move in the direction of the most good for the most people. No one knows what is best for the people except the people themselves. Sometimes peoples have forgotten that and yielded to "strong men" who seemed to know better what was best for them. In the end they have always suffered for their error. I emphasize that the choice of democracy as a pattern for group living is as important as the objectives themselves. Choice of pattern —democracy or autocracy, voluntarism or compulsion— has divided man into two camps since the day he first came on earth. Those of us who have fundamental faith in people, who believe in the worth of the individual, choose democracy. Cynicism regarding man and the belief that the "masses" should be "used" result in a philosophy of autocracy and dictatorship. America in 1776 chose the democratic road, politically and economically. We intend to keep on that highway.

It was inevitable that as our factory system developed there would arise the question of developing democratic forms of living in our new economic environment. Americans would not struggle for political democracy and then passively accept economic dictatorship. Man, sooner or later, would demand that democratic patterns of living be extended to his place of work where, incidentally, a good share of his life is spent. And that brings us to the major problem of the next decade. Is economic democracy possible in our modern mass-production society?

There is but one possible answer to this question and it lies in our fundamental philosophical outlook. We either believe in democracy or we don't. If we do, then we should proceed to develop harmonious and efficient *patterns* of democratic living in our workshops. And in doing just that, we shall resolve our industrial relations problem.

Saying that successful democratic *patterns* of living in our factories, mines, mills, and workshops is the answer to the labor-management problem does not, however, give us a panacea. Rather it brings us to the great problem of how to make industrial self-government function effectively. The problem of political self-government has been with us for some time. The problem of industrial self-government is new. Basically, however, it is the same type of problem. For self-government in any sphere depends upon individual intelligence and self-discipline. And self-discipline implies that all the individuals who make up the community are in agreement upon basic principles. The Ten Commandments, the Golden Rule—these are examples of agreement upon principles. No government could exist if its citizens were not in common agreement on fundamentals of sound living. Like all governments, industrial self-government is based upon such an understanding. Thus our quest for industrial peace is a search for principles of sound industrial living; principles that can be accepted by every participant in our industrial world; principles that shall guide the daily actions of labor and management.

That a common yardstick of values was an essential of self-government was pointed out at the turn of the century by that famed British jurist, Lord Moulton of Bank. He concluded, as a result of his vast legal experience, that the relations of man to man could be classified into three broad categories. First, there was the sphere of complete compulsion. Man was prohibited from thievery, murder, arson. These laws were definite. They regulated man's behavior through threat of punishment and penalty. And they were enforceable.

The second sphere, Moulton observed, was that of complete freedom. Here the individual could express his personal likes and dislikes. In this sphere man can perform without inhibition since his activity does not affect society. There is no need for regulation.

In between the spheres of external compulsion and complete freedom lies the third zone of human conduct. It is here that the individual cannot perform with complete freedom without hurting the group, and yet where complete compulsion cannot be applied if we desire to maintain and extend democracy. In this third sphere—and it expands in direct ratio to the expansion of self-government—human conduct is based upon individual internal discipline, a sense of right and wrong, good character, ethics, and morals. Man's conduct in this sphere is rooted in agreement upon the principles of sound living.

It is in this third zone of human conduct that we must find the industrial relations answer—industrial self-government. If we are to have industrial self-government the principles of constructive industrial living need to be enunciated and understood by the citizens of our industrial community. These principles must become the firm foundation of a national policy on labor-management relations. There is a need for principles and policy to serve as a compass in the wilderness of emotions, prejudices, and fossilized interests that dominate our labor-management scene.

There is a great deal of confusion on this matter of a national policy on industrial relations. Some people think that a conference of union and business leaders to discuss issues such as union shop, seniority, wages and grievance procedures can produce a national policy and industrial stability. They have the cart before the horse.

Policy based upon principles will not be achieved through conciliation and mediation. It takes more than a sitting around the table and compromising on positions. It is the formulation of a fundamental course of conduct based upon a realistic appraisal of the forces in industry. It is a mature sense of right and wrong that dictates proper action by management and labor in any situation. Policy is conscience. It is character. It is a guide to daily living in the labor-management world.

Management and labor have failed to achieve a satisfactory and workable relationship because they have been absorbed in the solution of daily issues. There is a need for both to do some thinking on fundamentals. Each side has been motivated by its own driving force. Each has thought that its motives are incompatible with the motives of the other.

Management's primary drive is profit—profit deriving from production. Mass production is the cornerstone of our modern factory system. Management can accept no policy on industrial relations that does not include ever-increasing productivity. There can be no "agreement upon principles" that does not include the principle of production.

On its side, labor is motivated by its drive for "rights of man" on the job. The union is merely the modern instrumentality through which the individual achieves this freedom. Thus labor can accept no "agreement upon principles" that does not wholeheartedly encompass the principle of the acceptance of the union, the individual's "freedom road."

On management's side there is the strong feeling that labor's fight for human rights in the factory is really a fight against productive efficiency.

On labor's side there is the strong feeling that management's fight for productive efficiency is really a fight against human rights in the factory.

Productive efficiency and personal freedom are not so incompatible as these extreme positions would indicate. It is possible to have production *with* freedom. In fact, we must have it, for in it lies our national policy on industrial relations. It is the common ground upon which labor and management can cooperate. In it lies our guide to action— our code for "good conduct." In it lies our "agreement upon principles," the essential for self-government.

Production With Freedom—these three words sum up the principles and policy that can bring harmonious and efficient *patterns* of democratic living to our workshops. It will grant civil liberties on the job. It will extend the worker's political freedom to the factory. It will give him a say in his own destiny, a sense of freedom. Further, production with freedom will promulgate productivity. It will reemphasize that production is the number one objective of our economy. It will declare that production and progress are synonomous. To make this national policy work, labor must accept productivity; management must accept the union. Both must learn to work efficiently in a new factory atmosphere. Production with individual freedom is the only way to permanently sound and peaceful industrial relations.

That we are far from production with freedom is best evidenced by our notions on what should or should not be done in industry. There is a widespread belief that the panacea for the ills of industrial relations is simply labor-management cooperation. This school of thought suggests that if both sides will be fair and honest and approach each other with the spirit of cooperation, all will be well. It would be a simple world indeed, if such a simple answer were all that is needed. Actually we may well ask, "Cooperation—for what?" Cooperation is not an end in itself. People do not cooperate in a vacuum. They do not cooperate for the sake of cooperating. They cooperate around some principles and for the attainment of some objectives. There can be no intelligent cooperation until those principles are enunciated and accepted.

At the other extreme is the belief of many people that a little legislation applied in the right places will solve anything. These people demand government curbs. Thus, they hope to get "responsible" unions and "principled" labor leaders. At the same time they protest that government is getting too powerful. Curbs are at best a negative approach.

In between the extremes of cooperation and curbs are many shades of opinion and belief. They all have in common the concept that "unions are all right, if they're run right." That's true of government, the church, the home; it is a generalization that will fit anything at any time.

These popular notions on the approach to the solution of industrial relations are not confined to the general public. One might expect from industry some sound answers based upon the realistic appraisal of their own situation and past experience. Yet what do we find? Industry has no labor policy.

This nation has a sincere admiration for the greatness of its industrial leadership. Our industrialists have provided the engineering genius, the daring, and the imagination that have made America's production the envy of the world.

But this same great leadership has failed on a crucial problem. They have used their ingenuity to solve problems of production, of cost, of raw materials, of marketing. On all of these points they have applied logic and reason. You would expect the same logic and reason in their labor relations. The average industrialist can speak on the evils of unions, the ogre of the closed shop, the lawlessness of the picket line, and the usurpation of management's rights. But he does not have an intelligent and sound policy on labor relations. He has not begun to approach the problem of "agreement upon principles."

This same criticism can well be applied to labor. What is labor's policy on management relations? On production? Intelligent labor will agree that its past policy has been a defensive one, dictated by its fight for survival. Labor has had to engage in bitter struggles. It had to fight for the right to organize. Today it is still engaged in bitter combat with some sections of business to establish and maintain its unions. These things have contributed to labor's lack of approach to "agreement upon principles."

Popular panaceas, irrational beliefs, emotions, and negative defenses will have to be supplanted by sound practice based upon principles of sound industrial living. These principles will recognize the worth of the individual and yet be in harmony with the forces that operate in our world of mass production.

The application of "production with freedom" is the solution to the labor-management problem. The acceptance of this common yardstick of values as our industrial way of life will contribute to a national unity and stability, solidly based upon individual free will. It will guarantee freedom in the factory and thus grant economic citizenship. Production with freedom is the full creative expression of individual personality in harmony with mass production and an ever-increasing per-man-hour productivity. It is the establishment of management's right to manage efficiently, and to contribute more and more goods to an ever-expanding economy. It is a system of everybody's personality and everybody's productivity. It will yield the individual the understanding so necessary to individual self-discipline—the key to successful industrial self-government.

This ideal in industry, production plus democracy, needs defining and understanding so that it may flourish and grow. We must spell out what we expect from the individual so that he can become a good industrial citizen.

CHAPTER II

LET FREEDOM RING!

A brick shattered the glass.

"They insisted on an open shop and now they've got one. It's wide open—not a window left in the place." It was 1934 in Toledo, Ohio, and the striking employees of one of that city's great corporations were demanding the right to unionize. These workers had decided that this time their attempts to organize would not be stopped.

The same thoughts were electrifying the working people of Akron, Flint, San Francisco, Detroit. From coast to coast, labor was demanding "freedom in industry." Industrial "despotism" was crumbling. Its end in democratic America was long overdue.

All America knew and understood the struggles that had won political democracy for the people of these United States. Very little of America knew and understood the battles that had been fought to extend that democracy to industry.

The advent of the corporation and mass production ended an era of individual ownership and individual relations between owner and worker. The corporation was group enterprise. Large-scale enterprise with top management growing ever more remote led inevitably to dictatorship and tyranny in industry, with arbitrary use and abuse of power. Each department of each plant became a small kingdom ruled by an industrial tyrant—the foreman or superintendent. His word was law. He was the prosecutor, the judge, the jury, and the executioner. He hired and fired as he pleased. He disciplined at will. He distributed or withheld favors, as his mood might indicate. Just as long as the department ran with some degree of efficiency, there was little interference by the front office.

This was not true of all industries, but of enough to generate explosive forces.

The individual worker in this atmosphere did as he was told. He was merely a humble subject in the foreman's kingdom. The worker was at the complete mercy of his boss. How closely this system of discipline by dictatorship resembled that of totalitarian states was described by a European university graduate to Clinton Golden and Harold Ruttenberg, CIO steel union officials. The student stated:

> The factory reminded me of a European dictatorial state, where bureaucrats plan and order, and citizens work and obey. The board of the company was the government, and the workers were the people, ruled through a centralized hierarchy of officials and controlled by a mechanized system of registration, bookkeeping, time cards, and punch clocks. Like citizens of authoritarian states, we did our individual assignments without knowing their purpose—the foreman was our supreme visible authority. With his superiors we did not communicate. And the president, with his board members and directors, sat high above us like an invisible, unapproachable God.

The worker was determined to change all this. He would not tolerate in mine and factory the very things he had bitterly fought in his community and nation. Freedom in the factory meant, for the worker, all those things that political freedom gave him on the outside. Pride, dignity, self-respect, the right to question—these things were worth fighting for. He knew that this was the difference between the slave and the freeman. He was determined to abolish industrial slavery. He insisted upon the recognition of his union. He wanted a collective bargaining contract. And was determined to accept nothing less. The contract, enforced by his union, was his bill of rights. He wanted industrial citizenship with its individual freedom.

Elmo Roper, conductor of *Fortune's* poll, recently surveyed labor opinion. His findings indicate just how deep-rooted are workers' desires for a Bill of Rights in industry. Roper states that labor wants security first. Not just the security of old age pensions or unemployment insurance, but the security of permanent work at reasonably high wages. The worker is tired of being the slave of insecurity. Then, the worker wants a chance to advance, some recognition for a job well done. Further, the worker desires to be treated as a person. Workers want to have a genuine responsibility and a stake in the enterprise itself. They want to feel that they are needed. Finally, they want a feeling of dignity. They want respect as individuals.

Elmo Roper's poll proves that wages alone will not bring tranquillity to the industrial scene. The worker wants decent living standards. But he also wants a sense of being important and useful. He resents being treated merely as a cog in a machine. His self-respect demands an end to the attitude, "You get paid to take orders; I'll do the thinking."

There is the story of the artillery sergeant. He was questioned by a new commanding officer, who wanted to know what his men were thinking. He was asked what he would most like to do. He replied, "Get to shooting that big gun!" The officer questioned further, "What would you most like to know?" The sergeant replied. "To know what I am shooting at." Again the commanding officer asked, "Next to that, what would you most like to know?" "To know that I am hitting what I am shooting at," was the sergeant's reply.

The American worker wasn't even in the position of the sergeant. Top management never came around to ask what he thought and how he felt.

Through the years the struggles of America's working men and women, although centering around issues of wages and hours of work, have been further motivated by the issue of personal freedom. As early as 1786 the printers in

Philadelphia struck for a weekly minimum wage of six
dollars. Strikes and lockouts were frequent during the next
eighty years. But they were only a dress rehearsal for a
violent class war that began about 1872 and continued
until the passage of the National Labor Relations Act
(Wagner Act) in 1935 and the establishment of our strong
modern industrial unions.

The battle for individual freedom in the workshop did not
assume its intense form until late in the nineteenth century.
Before that, the worker who was willing to fight for individual dignity left the factory and proceeded to the new
frontiers. There he could express his individuality. He
could be a respected citizen. With the closing of the
frontiers, the worker had no choice but to stay and fight.
Thus the tremendous unionization drives in the 1870's and
1880's made headway, and thousands joined the new
American Federation of Labor. In coal, steel, textile, and
railroad great struggles took place; and everywhere men
were attempting to establish unions.

America's industrial history from 1870 was bloody and
violent. It might well be termed "America's Sixty Years'
War." In many places the corporation had established a
state within a state. Some corporations maintained private arsenals and small armies. These bloody battles
resulted in many killings. Some of these killings were so
outrageous that they prompted public condemnation.
Governor John Turner of Illinois, after an investigation of
the murder of twelve coal miners in the Chicago Virden
Coal Company strike, stated: "I charge the owners and
managers of this company as being law breakers and
morally and criminally responsible for the bloodshed and dis-
grace to our state."

The battles and casualty lists of America's Sixty Years'
War are well documented in President Wilson's Commission
on the Causes of Industrial Unrest in 1912; in the Commission of Inquiry of the Inter-Church Movement on the Steel
Strike of 1919; in President Cleveland's Commission on the

Pullman Strike; and in the voluminous records of Senator LaFollette's Senate Sub-Committee on Civil Liberties, 1936–1940.

All wars are eventually terminated, and the peace treaties outline the new relationship of the combatants. America's Sixty Years' War was no exception. The peace treaty in this case was the National Labor Relations Act enacted by Congress in 1935. Earlier, in 1926, the Railway Mediation Act performed the same function for the railroad industry. Industry was told that the right of the worker to organize would be protected. Government machinery was established so that through the ballot box workingmen could gain recognition of their union. Freedom in industry officially became a permanent part of the American way of life.

The Wagner Act ended an era in American economic history—an era that had begun in 1786 with the first strike. As in England, Australia, the Scandinavian countries, or other countries where capitalism has flourished, labor history in our country can be divided into three periods. We had, first, our period of illegality. It was unlawful for workingmen to combine into unions. They were jailed for conspiring to raise wages and were accused of restraining trade. In 1842, the Massachusetts Supreme Court ruled, in the case of *Commonwealth v. Hunt*, that organizations of workingmen formed for the purpose of benefiting themselves by attempting to secure higher wages, shorter hours, and improved working conditions were lawful. That ended the era of illegal unionism.

After 1842 it was no longer a felony to join a union. But unions were merely tolerated. Employers were conceded the privilege of discouraging union organization. Men could be forced, as a condition of employment, to sign individual contracts stating that they would not join a union. Unions had not yet been accepted as an integral part of the economy. Where unions were recognized it was done in a spirit of accepting a necessary evil.

The Wagner Act, in 1935, ended the second period in our labor history and began the third. Unions are now officially encouraged by the Federal government. They are permanently woven into our economic fabric. The third period of our labor history, however, has just begun. Collective bargaining as a *modus vivendi* in our mass-production industries is new. Take General Motors. Their first national agreement was not concluded until shortly before the Second World War. During the war, government suspended collective bargaining. All in all, free collective bargaining has operated for only a short time in most of American industry. The long haul is still before us. How the union will fit into our economy will be determined in the next fifty years.

But one thing is certain. The union has become a new and permanent force in industry. It has established the group relationship between labor and management. It has become the modern instrumentality through which the worker exercises his inalienable rights in the factory. And the union is a "something new" that must be considered by the realistic management. Age-old concepts of employer-employee relations are crumbling. Industry can never return to the old relationship of boss and bossed. The worker is no longer a time-clock number. He is no longer an automaton who can be pushed or directed at will. He is now an individual with basic rights—basic rights including

JUSTICE: The elemental desire for fair play is satisfied. The arbitrary abuse of managerial power ends.

STATUS: Recognition of the individual as an individual is assured. A man is a man.

OPPORTUNITY: One's job becomes a career. The right to forge ahead is assured.

REWARD: There is a democratic dissemination of the fruits of production through increased wages and job security.

What does all this mean to management? The new situation, individual freedom through the union, brings up for reevaluation every management concept. Management must now operate its factory within the limits prescribed by the maintenance of the worker's human rights. Every phase of management is affected by this new vibrant force. Managerial practice must be altered in keeping with the new situation created by the establishment of freedom in industry.

This new situation is not fully understood by many industrialists. There has been a tendency to continue operating in the same old manner. Clashes have occurred. But, more and more, intelligent management realizes that new conditions call for new practices. They have started to think about this *new* labor relations problem. This thinking starts from the premise that there is no return to the old days of unilateral action. Managers are becoming aware that if they wish to achieve stable labor-management relations they will have to accept wholeheartedly the new order of individual rights in the factory. They are starting to develop new managerial techniques, based upon a philosophy of leadership through consent instead of compulsion.

There are, however, still a few businessmen and business groups who have "gone back into the hills" and continue, with guerrilla warfare, their fight against industrial freedom. They want to return to compulsion in industry. They hope that recent history is only an interlude. They think that America's Sixty Years' War will flare again if they can only maintain their firing. It is well for America that there are so few businessmen of this type. These men who put personal principles above the nation's welfare are no asset to our way of life. Like the dinosaur, who became extinct because he could not adapt himself to changing conditions, our guerrilla industrialist will soon disappear.

Most businessmen want to work with the union. Embracing the concept of freedom in industry, however, is not a simple matter. It calls for a mental revolution on the part of the executive. It calls for pioneering in new managerial territory. Time study, job evaluation, merit rating, in fact, all of management's techniques must be oriented to worker consent and participation. Managerial controls, if they are to operate efficiently in this new environment, must be humanized and democratized.

Some employers will say, "Yes, we accept the union, but we cannot accept checks on management. It's the principle of the thing." Experience has taught labor that talk of "principles" on the part of industry has sometimes been a cover for union busting and usually an admission that the employer has not grasped the concept of leadership through consent. It is management's responsibility, if it desires a healthy labor relationship, to remove completely from the industrial scene, that destructive and negative force—fear. And in particular, fear of union busting. There is no insurmountable issue of "management prerogative" if management convinces labor and the public that freedom in industry is fully accepted by them.

Management's right to manage, its prerogative, must be exercised in a new way. The problem is fundamentally that of leadership in a democracy—the maintenance of efficient production within a framework of the preservation of individual freedom. It is a problem of retaining human rights on the job and yet not undermining factory discipline. The solution calls for the elimination of dictatorial discipline and the substitution of democratic discipline. It means the replacing of tyranny by leadership. All this, at times, is very trying for management, but it is the only way. For management to say that it cannot manage this way is to admit that it has no faith in democracy.

For the union, the failure of honest attempts by management to create these new patterns of managerial authority can only bring industrial anarchy and eventually a return of industrial dictatorship. The union has a large stake in making efficiency and freedom compatible. In fact, the union has a heavy responsibility. To exercise freedom one must know its limitations. Freedom can be abused. The union cannot use its new freedom to undermine factory discipline. Liberty does not mean anarchy. Management must continue to exercise its managerial function. A plant cannot operate any other way. The union, therefore, must do all in its power to assist management in maintaining democratic discipline.

The union has another grave responsibility. The worker joins the union to achieve freedom in industry. If the union is to remain a vehicle for freedom it will have to guard against tyrannical practices of its own. Unless it does, it is doomed to the same fate as management dictatorship. The American Civil Liberties Union, a protector of unionism, has called the attention of the unions to some antidemocratic practices that threaten unionism. It states:

> The rule of force in industrial relations has been supplanted, with few exceptions, by the rule of law. It is essential, therefore, that trade unions which now receive governmental recognition and protection should respond by freeing themselves from any remnants of the autocratic practices that accompanied the era of industrial warfare.

Because the union speaks for human rights, it must be a custodian of liberties. It will have to guarantee not to abuse freedom within its own organization. It cannot remove the power of arbitrary authority from management and then exercise it itself. Freedom in the factory can flourish only with corresponding freedom in the union. That means free elections, regular conventions, constitutional rule, publication of financial statements, protection of minority rights, and all other practices that we associate with freedom and democracy. There can be no talk of freedom in industry if our unions are not also free.

Dictatorship in industry is giving way to democracy.

The worker, through his new instrumentality, the union, is becoming an individual. He can now meet his foreman on a man-to-man basis. No longer is the judgment of the departmental boss final and irrevocable. Each worker can now seek redress of any wrong. He can appeal decisions to higher authorities. He can ask questions and receive explanations. He can participate directly in determining those affairs that affect him. Prior to the union, such participation was suppressed and denied. Now the individual's creative urge is allowed to flourish. He gives vent to his ideas, his thoughts of what's right and what's wrong. He is able to exercise, in the factory, the inalienable rights of man. All this means industrial citizenship for Joe Worker. It means freedom in industry.

Freedom in industry is 50 per cent of a sound industrial code of conduct. It is one of two principles that must be accepted by every participant in the industrial community if there is to be self-government. It is an essential part of a common yardstick of values that must govern the daily activity of management and union. It is an integral half of the "agreement upon principles," which can be summarized in the phrase "production with freedom."

CHAPTER III

THREE MAGIC LETTERS: PMH

Production plus democracy should be our philosophy of industrial living. In the last decade there has been much talk of expanding democracy. There has been less talk of expanding production.

Productivity is the basis of the modern industrial society. Mass production, with constantly improving machinery and techniques for increased man-hour productivity, is the heart of our industrial body. Any permanent stability in the workshop will have to be in harmony with this fundamental fact. Just as labor will fight to the end any attempt to abrogate individual freedom, so management will fight any attempt to undermine any part of the system of mass production. Labor must recognize the full implications of the necessity for its wholehearted acceptance of this second half of production with freedom. Unless it does, there can be no hope for harmonious labor-management relations or for industrial self-government.

The acceptance by the union of mass production as a principle of sound industrial living necessitates a constructive union attitude on two subjects, management rights and productivity techniques. Unless management can manage, it cannot achieve production. Unless management can apply modern managerial techniques such as time and motion study, it cannot operate efficiently. But management tools, whether administrative rights or techniques, must be properly used, and above all not misused or abused.

When management talks about management rights, it is talking about production. Labor must recognize that management has an obligation to worry about its prerogatives. It is understandable that management may be apprehensive that the entrance of the union will disturb its basic drive for production. Here I do not refer to those guerrilla industrialists who are using a crusade for management's rights as a smoke screen for restoring industrial dictatorship. On the part of *sincere* management this talk of rights is the result of management's sometimes finding itself in a position where it cannot manage its plant. It cannot produce because of unfair and unsound union rules, regulations, and checks. In these cases, collective bargaining becomes an impediment to efficient production and precipitates industrial warfare. The union must be ever ready to assist in working out patterns of management authority that will give production plus democracy.

Most unions today will agree that technical advance is both inevitable and progressive. Few unions now stand in the way of mechanization. But while the bulk of unions agree to the introduction of new machines, they have not as yet grasped the fact that the acceptance of mechanization must include the acceptance of managerial controls. When unions oppose "on principle" management techniques for increased production they are in the same position as those unions that years ago opposed the automatic machine. The union cannot accept productivity without accepting productivity techniques. If the union does not accept all the aspects of productivity it can expect management to engage in an all-out fight. For example, proper time-study and production standards are essential to modern factory operation. They are as much a part of modern production as is electrification.

There is a small plant in a town in northwestern Ohio that manufactures lathe chucks. The owners have correctly maintained that their only basis for existence is a quality product at a competitive price. Certainly the average manufacturer buying lathe chucks would prefer well-known brands unless this company could undersell and maintain quality. The company is owned by two men who are students of modern management techniques. They understand that the amount of money paid to labor matters little as long as the company is competitive from a production standpoint. It makes no critical difference to this business whether their labor is paid one dollar or one dollar and a quarter per hour. The plant's life or death factor is man-hour productivity. In order to compete successfully, the owners suggested to their labor union the introduction of fair time study and an incentive plan. The union rejected the plan. Their argument: "against union policy." The company, the union, and the jobs of the men are headed toward oblivion because of this short-sighted policy. The company has no alternative but to wage war against the union.

The complete acceptance of industrial efficiency is essential to the resolution of labor-management conflict and the achievement of self-government. Production pegging and feather-bedding are obstacles to labor-management understanding. Unions must examine their work rules. They must also examine their interunion relations. There was a widely publicized story during the war that illustrates the type of union practice that may be of advantage to a few for awhile but hurts everyone for all time. It was reported that a seaplane tender, already launched and almost outfitted, was waiting for a Navy crew. Steam-fitters in the hold came upon a section of copper-nickel plate already installed. The leaderman—shipyard term for strawboss—snapped to his men "Rip it out! Them damn coppersmiths can't do our work!" The steamfitters cut the pipe out, tossed it in a scrap pile, then installed new pipe exactly like the job they had just yanked out. Dozens of such stories have made the rounds.

Differences between unions as to which group has the right to do certain kinds of work, as well as union restrictions, have contributed to industrial waste. Perhaps the whole picture was summed up best by the shipyard superintendent who said, "Suppose the restrictions under which we're trying to build ships applied to your automobile.

Say your motor needed overhauling. You'd have to call a pipe fitter to disconnect your fuel lines. Then you'd send for an electrician to disconnect the wires. A machinist would have to take the carburetor off. None of the three, however, could clean any of these parts; a laborer would have to do that. The pipefitter couldn't put a new bend in the copper gas line; he'd have to get a coppersmith. And your pipe fitter, your electrician, your machinist and the coppersmith would all need helpers to stand by."

Of course, these are extreme and unusual examples. Public opinion is forcing a change in such obvious and open waste. If this were the only type of production restriction, the problem could be easily met. It is the more subtle kind of antiproduction practice that needs fundamental change. Take the thinking of some members of the Glass Bottle Blowers Association. For many years they had an unwritten law that after a member of the union finished a bottle of beer, it was his duty to break the bottle and so provide employment for the bottle blowers. Later this strategy was supplemented by a drive against beer in cans, and all labor was asked to drink only beer in bottles, without regard for the brothers who made cans. This was matched by some locals of the United Automobile Workers who manufactured running boards. They asked all labor to buy only cars with running boards and thus hoped to stay the general adoption of the streamlined automobile.

This antiproduction thinking is also evidenced by the individual worker. In a certain large plant in Detroit a huge press stamped and formed sheet metal that went into one of the nation's well-known consumer products. One workman was given the task of turning out 100 pieces per hour and 800 pieces per day. After a few weeks on the job, he discovered that it was possible to stamp out and form two sheets of steel at the same time, and that, further, this could be done in one stroke of the press without injuring the press or the die. He proceeded to do this. By working slowly, he managed to keep working a total of six hours per day. The remainder of the time he would intermittently wander around the plant. One day the foreman observed the worker's slow production pace and asked how he could manage to meet schedules. The worker replied that he was turning out the production required by the company's time study, and that the foreman was mistaken about his wasting time. The union steward then instructed the worker to abandon his placing of two sheets in the press at the same time, and to go back to the one-sheet method. The steward was afraid the foreman might discover the method and would institute it on all the presses, which might result in more work at lower wages.

Driven by the specters of unemployment and speed-up, workmen hold back on output. This is understandable. Yet if something is wrong with the philosophy of dumping coffee into the sea, plowing under cotton, and slaughtering little pigs, so something is wrong with restricting factory production. Production holdbacks must become an "unfair practice." Labor must *help* stop the plowing under in the factory. The union must accept and educate its membership to accept, "on principle," that it is good unionism as well as good Americanism to believe in and to practice high productivity. This must be done without qualifications. Labor should continue to insist on solving the problems of more equitable distribution of goods and national income, but it cannot withhold endorsement of high productivity until its objectives in the distribution field are completely won. Certainly labor cannot increase its own share of goods by producing less. The Second World War forced all America to think in high-production terms. The necessities of victory caused labor to examine its production practices. Today more and more of labor are accepting productivity. They must continue to do so in the future. There can be no return to scarcity philosophies and practices. Such a return would be disastrous.

Management, too, has responsibilities in this matter of productivity. Albert Ramond, president of the Albert

Ramond and Associates, successor to the Bedaux industrial engineering firm, recently told an audience at the Town Hall in Los Angeles: "The unused manpower and equipment capacity in industry that can be laid directly at management's door adds up to a much greater total than the waste caused by 'feather-bedding' by workers."

Management inefficiency and waste are serious, not alone in themselves, but also because they contribute to labor's "what the hell" attitude on production. Where two motions are made when one is sufficient, where three steps are taken when two will do, where four men are employed to do the work of three, *there* management and labor must cooperate to change methods and practices.

Waste in industry, as estimated by numerous experts, amounts to more than 35 per cent. This waste, in a large measure, is due to management's failure to use modern efficiency techniques. The losses in productivity may be in such obvious forms as waiting around, excessive scrap, or idle equipment. But more often it comes from causes not so readily observed. There are innumerable causes of inefficiency: faulty tools, unbalanced operations, poor planning and scheduling, improper working conditions and assignments, and inadequate supervision, to mention but a few.

Low labor productivity is often times due to poor management. But efficiency losses do not necessarily imply poor management. It is just a case of not using the most modern techniques to determine the productivity that *can* be obtained. There is too much reliance on past performance—good, bad, or indifferent. While labor productivity must be increased through the elimination of feather-bedding and production pegging, management has the responsibility for improving its own controls and leadership. With proper labor-management cooperation, PMH (production per man-hour) can rise steadily. It can be done without speed-up and stretch-out. Management, by putting its own house in order, can help to insure labor's acceptance of productivity.

Ever-increasing productivity is not just a matter of *working harder*. It is primarily a matter of *working better*. Nothing is wasted—neither materials, nor machinery capacity, nor man power. Labor's advocacy of such a program has far greater implications than just union-industry peace. Productivity is vital to the achievement of genuine full employment with an ever-rising standard of life. Labor and management by working together toward lower production costs can help keep employment and wages on a high level.

This production for employment has been particularly emphasized by the British. Their government, in its recent White Paper entitled "Employment Policy," states:

> Employment cannot be created by an Act of Parliament or by Government action alone. The success of the Policy outlined in this paper will ultimately depend on the efforts of employers and workers in industry; for without a rising standard of industrial efficiency we cannot achieve a high level of employment combined with a rising standard of living.

Recently Sir Frank Platt headed a British Cotton Textile Mission to the United States. Its purpose was an inquiry into the PMH (production per man-hour) of America's textile mills. The mission found that the average American textile worker produces from one and one quarter to ten times as much in an hour as the average English worker. Sir Frank states that America's higher PMH is due primarily to the use of more modern machinery. He emphasizes, however, that machinery is not the whole story. Scientific management contributes much to this PMH.

America's standard of living depends greatly on PMH. Full employment without an ever-increasing PMH might well mean a share-the-poverty situation. It is possible to have high-level employment with everyone "employed" making mud pies. Employment is no end in itself. The object of high-level employment is more goods and services. Management must develop new methods of working with labor to contribute more goods at less cost. A high PMH is achieved by taking advantage of the advances of technology and other management techniques as rapidly as possible.

The management that fears overproduction and the worker who is afraid of accepting production because of the fear of unemployment should study the report of March, 1943, of the National Bureau of Economic Research. It is entitled *Employment in Manufacturing* 1899–1939. The bureau studied employment and output in a forty-year period and came to the conclusion that the large increases in employment took place in those industries in which there was an exceptionally *large decline in employment per unit of product*. The automobile industry is cited as the outstanding example of this trend. It *cut jobs per unit most sharply and yet registered the largest gain in employment*. This fact indicates clearly the tie-up between high-level employment and high-level productivity. In contrast, the lumber industry *increased its employment per unit of product*. The Bureau records that the lumber industry suffered a *sharp reduction in both total employment and total output.*

The Ford Motor Company has compiled some interesting facts and figures on the production of the inner shell of the hubcap of its 1938 Ford car. These hubcap shells cost a little over twelve cents apiece. They are turned out on an automatic press. High PMH produces 2,160 hubcap shells in the same length of time as it takes a handworker to pound out *one*. There are some who might argue that this productivity has eliminated 2,159 possible jobs. The facts indicate otherwise. The hubcap shells, produced by hand, would cost $2.50 each. Pretty high for an article that can be made for twelve cents!

The argument might continue, however, that the higher cost of hand production should be paid in the interests of employing those 2,159 men. But would the higher price be paid? If the principle of low productivity were followed in all operations in the manufacture of an automobile, there would be few cars sold. It is calculated that the cost of producing a 1938 Ford on this hand basis would have been $17,850. At such a price, not fifty cars a year would be sold. There would not be work for *one* of those 2,160 men who were "displaced" by ever increasing productivity. Without high productivity there would be no automobile industry with its hundreds of thousands of jobs.

Productivity means more goods for more people. Labor and management must eradicate waste. They must tackle *every phase* of the problem. They must achieve a high production per man-hour. This means the utilization of the energy of every individual. Everyone who can contribute to the total production must be given a chance to do so. *The standard of living of every American is lowered when some Americans are excluded from contributing to the production of our total wealth.* This is a phase of waste that has not been met squarely. If the concept of high-level production is to be accepted, then the Negro, the Mexican, in fact every American must be given an opportunity to *produce at his greatest skill.*

During the war, the Federal government addressed a question to war-goods manufacturers: "How many of your new jobs will be open to Negroes?" The replies showed that 51 per cent of those new jobs, skilled or unskilled, would be closed to Negroes. Why? Just curtly and brutally, "Employment policy."

Important unions join important employers in that policy. All five of the great unions that operate our railroad trains—engineers, firemen, conductors, trainmen, switchmen—deny membership to Negroes. They sometimes go further. The railroad unions have no "closed shops" and thousands of Negroes work as firemen and trainmen on railroads in the South without being union members. They have done it for a long, long time. Now the white "brothers" representing "humanity" are trying to drive those Negroes out of their jobs.

Early in this century, the unionized white trainmen and firemen in the South began to negotiate collective-bargaining agreements with railroad managements, confining Negroes to certain percentages of the total number of trainmen and firemen employed. They have continuously and ruthlessly reduced these percentages. In 1910, 30 per cent of all trainmen in the South were Negroes; in 1940, only 15 per cent. In 1910, 41 per cent of all firemen in the South were Negroes; in 1940, only 29 per cent. At the present pace there will be no Negro trainmen or firemen left in the South by 1960. The whites will have robbed the Southern Negro of one of their most ancient industrial occupational heritages. How does this fit in with a policy of productivity?

Our 13,000,000 American Negroes are not today the national economic asset that they could be. To develop them into being that asset, to the utmost of their capacity, is only solid economic common sense. PMH demands "no discrimination" in industry. In this world we need all the working energy, male or female, of whatever racial or national origin, that we can assemble. Every ounce of such energy used is a national gain. Every ounce of it not used is a national loss.

The all-out acceptance of productivity as the key to America's dream of a good life is also urged by the scientists. While we are concerned with production and its effect on our times, scientists have studied production and its effect on man's status from the days of his origin.

Professor Leslie White, anthropologist at the University of Michigan, has studied in detail the subject of productivity and civilization. Professor White points out that man would have remained on the level of savagery indefinitely if he had not increased his per capita productivity. The amount of energy used per person in the earliest stage of civilization was very small indeed. White develops a general law of our development and concludes that, other things being equal, civilization evolves as the productivity of human labor increases. Science discloses that the forward march of man is dependent upon productivity.

In this country we harness electrical, mechanical, and other forms of energy equivalent to one hundred human slaves for each of us. In England the energy used is about half of ours, and in China about one twenty-fifth. This accounts in large part for the difference in living standards in each country. American PMH has made possible the low cost auto. There are millions of car owners in America. The British worker rides his bicycle. Scientists all agree that our material progress is limited only by our productivity.

There is still another aspect of the acceptance by labor of productivity. Union advocacy of productivity is good collective bargaining. An objective of negotiations with management has always been the raising of the living standards of the union membership. The union, through the bargaining table, attempts to increase wages. It desires to redistribute the proceeds of the company's sales dollar. In the early stages of collective bargaining the union feels that the only way to increase wages is to decrease profits. Actually, many firms continue to earn the same profit after union recognition and wage increases. Sometimes the wage increase is reflected in price increase. More often, under pressure of increasing labor cost, firms eliminate waste and increase productivity. Thus they reduce labor cost per unit and maintain their profit structure in the face of rising wages.

A time comes, however, when wage demands will outstrip immediate productivity increases. Then living standards of labor are improved at the expense of the corporation's profit margin. This improvement means a larger share of the national income for labor and less for capital. Eventually, in a profit system, such redistribution of national income reaches a stabilization point. Capital, on its side, demands a reasonable return. Living standards of labor, therefore, cannot be indefinitely increased merely by income redistribution.

Ultimately there is only one way to increase labor's material goods. That is to produce more. The quickest way to more pie is to bake a larger pie. Ever-increasing productivity will mean that one hour's work can buy two shirts where it would only buy one before. Ever increasing productivity will mean more and more goods reaching more and more people.

Union bargaining will eventually come up against the reality that the one way to improve the economic position of the worker is—more and more production. At the present time our PMH is increasing at the rate of approximately 3 per cent per year. It is this steady productivity advance that determines our standard of living. It is good unionism, from every angle, wholeheartedly to accept productivity.

"Productivity" has been a much used word in this chapter. This has been necessary because the nation's welfare makes it imperative that labor and industry understand why they must work together for it. I have maintained that industry will have to accept the concept of freedom. I maintain with equal fervor that labor will have to accept the concept of productivity. Together, freedom and production form our "principles" upon which agreement is necessary if the inhabitants of our industrial community desire successful self-government.

CHAPTER IV

LEGISLATIVE-EXECUTIVE-JUDICIAL

"Mike has tended that furnace for sixteen years, and no two-bit sawbones is going to keep him off that job."

"That's what you think; we're running this plant and what we say goes. Mike is not coming into this plant until our doctor says he's ready to work."

"Your company-stooge Doc wouldn't know a sick man if he bumped into one. I wouldn't trust him with my Airedale. Mike's family doctor says he's fit to work, and by God he's going to."

The chief steward, the elected spokesman of the men, was pounding the table. His face was flushed and he was getting angrier by the minute. The works manager was in the same mood. This was not the first time that the issue of medical examinations had precipitated angry words. It was the kind of debate that resulted only in frustration on both sides. It always led to that stonewall—"company policy."

Sometime before this incident of Mike's return to work, the company had announced one day that all employees who were absent for more than one week would have to be examined by the firm's physician, in order that fitness for reemployment might be determined. This statement caused no immediate upheaval. It was not until the company doctor refused to permit Mary to return to her job that the unrest started. The company doctor claimed that she had a tumor. Mary's family doctor said she hadn't. Management and union violently discussed the case. They reached no conclusion.

The very next day Bertha was told she couldn't work on her high-paying job because she had arthritis. Her doctor said, "Yes, she has arthritis, but it won't interfere with

32

her work." The works manager and the chief steward went round and round on that case. Neither side could see any possible compromise.

The days went on. Although there weren't too many cases, there were enough to start plant talk. "The company is weeding out the old-timers.—The company is getting rid of the good union people.—The company doesn't want to pay compensation.—The same old company tricks, but this time they're hiding behind sawbones."

The barring of Mike from his job was the last straw. Mike had sixteen years of seniority. His job as furnace tender was tough and hot, but it paid well. There had been rumors that the company would like to get rid of the seniority clause in that department. It was said that the company wanted younger men on the furnace jobs. The old-timers were burnt out. They were ready for the scrap heap. When the company doctor told Mike he had a bad heart and could not return to his furnace, every worker in the plant walked out, feeling that the company had "pulled a fast one on poor old Mike—anyone of us might be next."

With their employees on strike, in spite of the no-strike clause in the union contract, the company decided that collective bargaining just didn't work. The company officials pointed to the record. Hadn't they allowed free expression of all grievances? Hadn't they discussed the grievances resulting from medical examinations? Hadn't they patiently given their time to listen to arguments from the union?

The union members on the picket line felt grievously hurt. In spite of the contract, they reasoned, this company just didn't want to bargain collectively. Pretty smart company. Just let the union talk and talk—blow off steam. Then answer, "nothing can be done on this matter—company policy." Like batting your head against a stonewall, trying to buck company policy.

The shutdown had occurred because neither side realized

that it is impossible to settle policy matters through grievance machinery. Fortunately this impasse was not ended by another "power compromise" or "middle-of-the-road" arbitration. The company president left his New York office and went out to Mill Town. The company had sincerely accepted the union. It had signed a contract. It had discussed grievances and had attempted to settle them. The president was determined to learn the "why" of this continuous strife between management and union.

Upon arrival the company president called in the local bargaining committee. He asked, "Why the walkout?" The union committee unfolded their story. They didn't intend to stand by and see their old-timers slowly weeded out. They felt that there had to be a showdown on the issue. The company president felt relieved—so, that was all that was wrong. He pointed to the seniority clauses. Hadn't the company indicated its intention to keep old-timers at work when it agreed to seniority? Why, the company had never harbored a single thought about eliminating older employees. It had instituted the medical reexamination in the best interests of the employees. There were certain work conditions and hazards that were fatal to definite types of illness. A heart condition and furnace work just didn't go together, bad for the worker and hazardous for his fellow workers. Weren't bus drivers with bad hearts and high blood pressure banned from driving and transferred to other jobs, in the interests of safety? "Actually," the company chief stated, "our intentions are strictly honorable."

Company and union then proceeded to do what should have been done in the first place. They proceeded really to *bargain collectively*. Company policy on medical examinations was reviewed. The company stated its objectives and program and asked for comments. A detailed discussion took place. Provisions were agreed upon. Under certain circumstances employees would be transferred to suitable work, with protection of seniority. In cases where family doctor and company doctor disagreed, the local university hospital would make the final medical diagnosis. Types of physical defects and kinds of jobs that would prevent employment of individuals with those afflictions were listed. The complete policy was then submitted to the union membership for discussion and vote. It was adopted and became a part of the code of conduct in the plant.

Now the prerequisites for the settlement of grievances arising from medical examinations had been laid. Company policy affecting worker welfare had been democratically determined. Manager and union steward could discuss the merits of an individual case against the background of the predetermined code of conduct. Grievances would be confined to charges of *maladministration* of policy. Such grievances can be easily judged and quickly disposed of on the basis of fact.

Collective bargaining is not a mere signing of an agreement granting seniority, vacations and wage increases. It is not a mere sitting around the table discussing grievances. Basically, it is the democratic, joint formulation of "company policy" on *all* matters that directly affect the worker in the plant. Collective bargaining is self-government in operation. It is the projection of policy by management with labor given a right to be heard. It is the establishment of factory law based upon common consent.

This joint approach to the formulation of factory law is the key to successful plant labor-management relations. This approach, however, will succeed only if both sides have accepted the philosophy of sound industrial living— production with freedom. Production with freedom is, in essence, a *technique of approach* to every policy problem confronting the local management and union. It is the yardstick that determines "right" or "wrong."

Take the company confronted with the problem of increasing production. It desires to institute a policy of incentive payments (or monetary inducements for above normal production). Top management meets with the union. Management outlines the desired objectives and procedures. A complete discussion takes place. "Production plus democracy" guides both sides. The union agrees that high productivity is necessary but asks that the incentive policy incorporate certain rules to protect the individual's earnings, health, and work standards. Management accepts the suggested safeguards. The new incentive policy as amended in no way impairs the basic objectives of increased production and yet embodies individual rights.

Upon completion of the statement on incentive policy and program, the entire matter is submitted to a secret rank and file vote. Through meetings and pamphlets, every individual is informed of all details. He asks questions and he receives answers. The vote carries and the plan is adopted. The incentive system becomes factory law. This is successful collective bargaining. This is good labor relations. It is intelligent human relations. It is "production with freedom" in action.

This union participation in policy determination does not conflict with management's basic right to manage. There is a need for a clarification of thinking on this issue of management's rights. That management which guards its "rights" and states that it will not be "dictated to" usually means that it will not cease to dictate. Much of the confusion on this issue of prerogatives results from the tendency to discuss management's rights as if they exist in a vacuum.

Through the years the concepts of management's function are constantly being modified and changed as the production environment changes. There is a logical inconsistency in treating rights as unchangeable. New rights are continually being formed and others are continually breaking down. Thus the entrance of the union requires a new kind of exercise of management rights.

In the past it was generally considered management's prerogative to formulate all factory law. This included all rules and regulations, hours of work, working conditions, and wage payments. Take the right of layoff. Twenty years ago management was the sole judge of whom to layoff if business receded. Now there are seniority lists in all organized and in most unorganized plants. Management has conceded that layoffs should be governed by fair rules. It is a rare management today that argues that it alone should decide who shall remain at work. Thus we see that what was once an unassailable management prerogative has changed with changing times. And this is true of all management rights. They change as the production environment changes.

At this point management asks, "Where does labor participation in policy making stop? Won't this situation lead to a complete usurpation of management rights?" That management which argues the matter of labor participation in policy making from the standpoint of "where to draw the line" misses the point entirely. Management should ask questions, but not on "where to draw the line." The intelligent management ought to ask, "Has labor accepted production with freedom as its basic approach to participation?" Unless labor has, participation will not be successful for there is no common yardstick of values. Management through compulsion should give way to management by consent, but that kind of leadership can work only if those who are consenting are in agreement with the leaders on fundamental concepts of right and wrong.

Management also ought to ask, "Does this particular case of participation by labor undermine our leadership in the plant?" Note that participation in policy making will destroy *dictatorial* leadership but it does not have to destroy *leadership*. The basic right that management must guard is its authority to direct if it is to continue to lead. And it must lead if the plant is to operate efficiently.

While management rights will be modified and changed as time goes on, there must be no infringement by labor on management's basic right to direct and administer. Thus, while labor participates in policy making, it does not participate in management. There is no sharing of leadership, direction, or administration. This is the essential difference between participation in policy making and participation in management.

Applying this right of management direction to the practical problem of factory operation, we find that management must retain the power, within a democratic frame of reference:

To hire
To fire
To assign work
To direct the working force
To discipline
To promote to managerial positions
To administer every management technique necessary to production
To bring together men, materials, and equipment in efficient production
To determine sales and price policies

Management that fears labor participation in policy making will get all the disadvantages of a union and none of its advantages. Labor participation and consultation means the active support of the worker in helping to solve management problems. It further means the full utilization of the creative energies of the labor force.

Production with freedom clearly defines the spheres of activity and responsibility of both labor and management. Labor's acceptance of productivity carries with it the recognition of management's managerial role. Management's acceptance of freedom carries with it the recognition of the union's function to complain and to seek redress of wrongs within a jointly predetermined code of factory law.

A parallel can be drawn between self-government in the political sphere and self-government in our economic life.

We have established three branches of government. The legislative, the executive and the judicial are our democratic political patterns. Collective bargaining—self-government in our factory community—can operate the same way. Thus we find:

THE LEGISLATIVE: Management and labor discuss and determine factory law. This might also be called labor participation in policy making.

THE EXECUTIVE: This is management's exclusive sphere of operation. Factory law is administered by management.

THE JUDICIAL: This is the grievance procedure with arbitration. Here labor may present its complaints if it feels that management has maladministered factory law.

The legislative, the executive, and the judicial establish constitutional government in industry. They outline clearly labor's and management's functions. The union does not participate in managing the plant. It does participate in formulating factory law. It does check on the administration and application of that law by management. The union steward does not assume management's functions in any way. He is interested, however, in fair and accurate application of the jointly determined policy.

The sound union-management relationship provides the machinery through which every worker maintains his democratic right of seeking redress of wrongs. Every worker has the right to an answer. He seeks that answer through the grievance machinery. His grievances, however, are limited to a maladministration or misapplication of the jointly formulated factory law. This procedure puts "facts in the saddle." A quick determination of the justness of the claim is possible. The issue is free from emotion and can be settled on its merits. The worker does not present grievances on whether the basic policy should or should not be pursued. That discussion has been held. It cannot be reopened every day or anarchy will prevail. As factory law based upon contract and agreed-upon policy (the legislative) is accumulated, fewer and fewer grievances present themselves. More and more, the foreman, the steward, and the worker settle into a pattern of democratic plant life free from violent bickering and bitter strife.

One more point should be made. The peaceful plant relationship requires provision for outside arbitration on those issues that cannot be settled by the union and management. An analogy can be drawn between the modern factory and the community. Orderly behavior in the community is dependent upon the acceptance by each citizen of court system. The citizen has faith in achieving justice through the court. He does not have to resort to "might makes right." In the early frontier towns sufficient confidence had to be built in the orderly process as a method of obtaining justice before the court replaced the gun. The peaceful operation of the factory also requires a building of confidence in the orderly process. Order is based upon the faith of the individual that outside arbitration, as the ultimate step in the grievance procedure, will assure just application of factory law. Arbitration is the entrance of the court system of judge and jury into the industrial world. Without this court no civilized community can exist. The possibility of impartial arbitration will create the "law-abiding" industrial citizen.

We have outlined the principles of peaceful labor-management relations. *Peaceful* collective bargaining, however, does not necessarily mean *constructive* collective bargaining. Collective bargaining, in and by itself, is no permanent solution to our industrial relations problem. The permanent solution is only collective bargaining within the framework of our basic philosophy of production with freedom. Some of the experiences of the building trades illustrate this point. There we find harmonious collective bargaining. Labor-management strife has been eliminated. Collective bargaining in some parts of the construction industry has become collusive bargaining.

During 1939, a prewar year, the Federal Home Loan Bank Board published building-activity figures of selected American cities. These figures indicated that there was fourteen times as much residential housing construction in Los Angeles as there was in Cleveland. The Cleveland building-trades artisans have done much more collective bargaining than the building trades artisans of Los Angeles. That is their right and they have exercised it. Throughout the city they are unionized. Throughout the city they enjoy a completely closed shop. This high degree of collective bargaining without the production-with-freedom approach may have accounted for the lack of home building in the city of Cleveland.

The Department of Justice has investigated this kind of collective bargaining. Contracts have been gathered from all corners of the country. From these, William Hard, noted writer, put together a perfected peak specimen of the sort of contract signed by many associations of building-trades employers and many unions of building-trades employees.

The employers, in order to please the union, agree to such things as the following:

They will not require the use of spray-paint guns and will cause all painting to be done by the slower and more expensive method of the hand brush.

They will not accept finished floor boards; or, if the floor boards arrive with a finish on them, they will hire workmen to take the finish off and put it on again.

They will not hire common laborers to unload trucks of plumbing materials but will cause that common labor to be done by high-priced skilled plumbing artisans.

They will not allow any lather to nail lath to the top of his capacity, but will keep him down to a specified number of laths a day.

They will not listen to any architect who might say that one coat of plaster will do, but will hire plasterers to put on three coats, etc., etc., etc.

Meanwhile, and in return, in order to please the employers, the union members agree to such things as the following:

They will refuse to work for any employer who for any reason is not accepted as a member of the association of employers.

They will refuse to work on any materials that have not received the approval of the association of employers.

They will refuse to work on any job where the contract has been secured through a bid that the association of employers regards as too low.

They will refuse to work directly for any householder and will work only through a contractor, with the contractor, getting his profit and paying dues to the association of contractors, etc., etc., etc.

William Hard points out that Cleveland has labor-management peace in the building industry, but it is the peace of the graveyard. It is collective bargaining based upon scarcity economics. The building industry, employers and employees, need a code of conduct embodying production with freedom.

I have said that collective bargaining is industrial self-government. But the existence of self-government depends upon an educated citizen. This raises the question as to responsibility for the education of our industrial citizens. Too many managements feel that with the advent of the union their responsibility for employee attitudes is finished. Thus management withdraws from the field and curtails its personnel activity precisely at a time when it should be increasing it. Management cannot escape the effects of employee attitudes just because the union has entered the picture. Management must intensify its program for achieving constructive worker attitudes. But it must do it in a new way—in cooperation with the union.

Personnel practices must now be reoriented. Too much of management's past activity in the field of employee attitudes has been aimed at union "busting" instead of at sound principles. There is a mistaken notion abroad that to achieve worker confidence in management—an objective of sound personnel practice—one must destroy worker confidence in unionism; that to achieve worker cooperation in increasing output one must eliminate the union. I maintain that modern personnel practice will be conducted through and with the union on the basis of production and democracy. It will either be done that way or it will not be done at all. The intelligent management will adapt itself to new conditions and proceed to new personnel techniques. The goal of a cooperative worker remains whether or not the union is present.

Take the example of the Libbey-Owens Ford Glass Company. A strike shut down its plants for several months in 1946. Yet at the termination of that strike, employees were welcomed back to work by a joint union-company letter. The letter stated, in part:

We, as officials of the union and the company, are all thankful that the glass strike is ended. We will all do everything possible in the future to avoid a repetition.

The company is glad to have you back at work in its factories. The union and each of you individually are assured of the good will of the company. The union likewise assures the company of its good will and cooperation.

For years the management has been working on new and expanded uses for glass. Today many of them are a reality. The demand for glass in the building field, in the automotive industry, in fact in all lines, seems greater than ever before. There is plenty of work. Maximum output during these next few months will protect our industry against inroads from new competitive materials and thus better insure your jobs far into the future.

Cooperation between men and management will insure good production. Good production is the best possible insurance of good wages. You, the union and the company, are a team in this industry. We lose ground or succeed together.

This is the new personnel approach. It is a policy of getting sound employee relations adapted to a new industrial environment—an environment in which the union plays an important part.

It is an approach that acknowledges that the labor force is an entity represented by the union. It is the approach that recognizes that the individual is reached through the union and not around it. It is this concept—the labor force as an entity—that differentiates the new personnel practices from the old. Management must adjust its thinking so that all of its human relations activity is pitched on the note of its employees as an entity. I emphasize that the concept of the labor force as an entity must underlie *all* management activity, not just that portion that falls within the scope of collective bargaining.

This kind of union-management relationship, with its worker participation in every phase of factory life, along with the retention by management of its power of initiative, provides the foundation for harmonious employer-employee relations. Worker participation leads to worker cooperation—a prerequisite if our productivity potential is to be realized.

Collective bargaining, like democracy, is only a technique. It can be good or bad. If the technique is used by men who are grounded in the concept of production plus democracy, then collective bargaining is constructive. Constructive collective bargaining can become our industrial way of life. First, however, production with freedom will have to become the mind and conscience of every individual in our industrial world.

CHAPTER V

FROM COLLECTIVE BARGAINING TO COOPERATIVE PLANNING

America learned many things from the Second World War. A most important discovery was that management and labor can perform production miracles—*if they cooperate*. Wartime production experience indicates that a tremendous potential of increased productivity exists. It can be realized through a teamwork approach. When the brains and energy of labor are added to the brains and energy of management, improved production is inevitable.

Government, seeking to utilize this production potential, established within the War Production Board a division whose sole function was stimulation of teamwork in the factory. Management and labor were asked to set up production committees. Numerous pamphlets, posters, and leaflets were distributed to the nation's workshops to bring about full worker participation in the production process. By the end of the war there were in existence more than 5,000 labor-management production committees covering some 8,000,000 workers. These joint committees were meeting regularly on the direct and indirect problems of production. They were discussing quality, improvement, waste elimination, and better work methods. While some committees did not live up to expectations, enough of them recorded sufficient achievement to indicate the tremendous possibilities inherent in the approach.

Typical of the industrial leaders who accepted the concept of labor's creative participation in the production process was Cyril Bath, president of the Cyril Bath Company, Cleveland manufacturers. He stated: "I am personally very sure that the Labor-Management Production Committee Campaign is tapping a source of greatly increased production that needs neither plant, tools, nor capital."

Similar statements were issued by more than one hundred leading industrialists. All of them agreed with C. E. Wilson, General Electric president, who proclaimed the advantages of "management and labor pooling their knowledge and experience to make a common attack on problems of production."

The response from some of the nation's employers was enlightened and impressive. Labor-management committees were set up not only in struggling firms but in many of the most strongly established corporations in the country. They included such companies as: United States Steel, Goodyear Rubber, Remington Arms, Aluminum Company of America, Corning Glass, Chrysler, North American Aviation, National Cash Register, Armstrong Cork, Bendix, Allis-Chalmers, Revere Copper, International Business Machines, Johns-Manville, Caterpillar Tractor, Eastman Kodak, American Locomotive. The du Pont Company, one of America's oldest industrial organizations, established management-labor committees in twenty-five of its plants.

The wartime labor-management production committees had as their prime purpose the stimulation of favorable employee attitudes on increased output. The committees knew that big economies in time and material come from a series of little economies. These little economies can best be made by the individual on the job. He is in the best position to view his own immediate work. Many times these small savings are beyond the attention of the manager and the engineer who are absorbed by a daily routine of "big" production problems. Yet this field of small economies contains unlimited possibilities for those interested in efficiency advance.

The various wartime committees proceeded in different ways. Some production committees concentrated on getting workers to think about their work and better work methods. Everybody in the plant began to ask, "Why?"

These "whys" produced some sublime headaches—and some very red faces now and then—for top management. Typical of stories reported was that of the du Pont Company's pigment plant in Wilmington, Delaware. In this plant there was a dry room and a grind room. Barrels of pigment were always weighed as they went from one room into the other. A workman inquired: "*Why* do we weigh those barrels of pigment?" Top management plunged itself into profound thought. When it emerged, it said, "There is no reason whatsoever." So the weighing of the barrels was abolished and much time saved.

Take the production committee of the Plomb Tool Company of Los Angeles. It developed worker participation in increasing productivity by suggesting self motion study. The committee issued an illustrated pamphlet and asked each employee to improve his efficiency through a study of his own efforts and methods. Scientific methods analysis was reduced to simple language and pictures. Every worker studied his job. He asked such questions as "Is this motion necessary? Could it be shortened or performed with less effort if the work were rearranged? Can one or both hands be freed from holding the work by some clamp or fixture operated by the foot?" The Plomb Tool Company reported increased production per manhour (PMH) as each worker reduced the time and effort necessary to complete the job.

Hundreds of such incidents could be given. Consider the girl in the Richmond plant of Larus & Brother, tobacco manufacturers. She stood beside a system of belt conveyors on which cartons of cigarettes were traveling. At a certain point they had to be turned so that they would travel head-on. The girl was energetically doing the turning. She was also asking herself, "Is this way the easiest?" Her foreman also wondered whether the turning could be done better and cheaper. He decided to build a machine to do the turning. The machine would cost about $300. The next day he walked up to the girl to discuss the project. He noticed that she didn't seem to be working. However, the first finger of her right hand was projecting about an inch over the belt conveyor. The foreman was amazed. The girl had found the strategic spot. Each carton, as it struck her finger, swerved exactly right and went its way head-on. That girl had reduced work to motionlessness. A nail was installed where she had held her finger. The nail turned the cartons, and in this case, the girl was free for another and better-paying job in the plant.

The Westinghouse Company and the CIO Electrical Workers Union did an excellent job on waste elimination and quality improvement. And their experience has not been restricted to wartime. As far back as 1937, they established departmental efficiency committees. At the Springfield, Massachusetts plant there are some 5,000 employees. Those men and women participate in advancing production through top committees, division committees, and forty-six departmental committees. There are over 200 labor members on the various committees.

Management reports excellent productivity progress. Each year, labor and management choose a special project for concentrated effort. In 1942 the central theme of all committee meetings was material conservation. Ideas were exchanged on ways to use scrap ends of stock that normally would have been discarded. In that year one department alone salvaged 25,000 pounds of aluminum, 22,992 pounds of steel, 57 pounds of copper, and 112 pounds of brass. What a tremendous saving of raw material and natural resources if this record were equaled in every factory!

Where human energy is used in the production process it is obvious that the introduction of better work methods will increase productivity. Efficiency advances resulting from labor-management cooperation are more difficult in those industries that are highly mechanized. Chemical manufacture is that kind of industry. Yet, excellent results from the joint approach was reported by the Monsanto Chemical Company.

Some 1,500 employees of Monsanto Chemical are members of the AFL Chemical Workers Union. The company and the union established twenty-two departmental committees. Their record was excellent. In one department alone a startling increase in output from 450 to 1,100 tons per month was established. This increase was made by small degrees over a period of time by suggestions from everyone in the department.

Besides the really large production increases at Monsanto there were numerous small economies. Typical was a change in rules to permit laborers to ride the trucks to where shoveling had to be done. Formerly, trucks had to await the arrival of the laborers, who had to walk. The simple change in rules suggested by the committee saved valuable time and energy.

There are hundreds and hundreds of reports on the accomplishments of labor-management committees. While the committees have differed on organizational structure and specific activities, all of them agreed that the joint approach to efficiency got results. This was all done under the high impetus of the war—patriotism—the urge to serve.

Probably the most sceptical industrialist, as a result of these wartime experiences, is now reconsidering his position on worker participation in efficiency advance. General Motors, among others, did not establish labor-management production committees during the war. They did, however, tap the mental resources of their employees. T. P. Archer, vice-president, reports that in 1941 the company introduced a suggestion-award system. In two years 180,000 ideas were submitted by their 400,000 workers. Of these suggestions, 33,831 were acceptable. One out of five ideas had some merit and was used. That the ideas were worth while is evidenced by the $1,214,000. that was paid out in awards.

These suggestions, covering every conceivable subject, resulted in real savings in man power and materials. Out of General Motors thirty-six divisions, it was found that in one division alone 350,000 man-hours were saved. Of the ideas submitted, 140 were good enough to merit the top award of $1,000 each. But General Motors just scratched the surface of worker ideas. Its suggestion system was only a beginning, because it had no provision for genuine worker participation through a union-management arrangement.

There is no doubt that the individual worker has much to contribute to industry. Management, however, will have to encourage worker creativeness. Suggestion systems are the first step. Labor-management production committees are the next. The ultimate and best form, however, is the approach that uses foreman and steward for *day-to-day* efficiency advances. Fundamentally, however, this entails understanding production with freedom with its complete acceptance of the union by management and the acceptance of production by the union. Only then can there be that joint venture of foreman and steward for productivity increases. The foreman, whose main responsibility is production, then begins to see that the acceptance of human rights in the plant is the road to higher and higher production goals. Recognition of individual worth releases the creative energies of workers. Foremanship becomes democratic leadership.

The steward, whose principal activity has been the protection of individual liberties, becomes production-minded. Foreman and steward each sees that production goals and human rights cannot be separated. They start to work as a team in the department. The foreman and the steward become the front-line advocates of "scientific" management, of an ever-rising efficiency standard, and of the utilization of every individual's brain as well as brawn. The foreman-steward relationship is no longer confined to grievance discussions. Production problems receive more and more attention at their get-togethers. Genuine teamwork is achieved.

The necessity for a constructive foreman-steward relationship cannot be overemphasized.   The foreman and the steward are each key men in his respective organization. To the men in the department, the foreman *is* the company. His actions, his thoughts, his methods, are the basis for whatever opinion the worker forms of the firm.   The steward is the union equivalent of the company foreman. He is the departmental union chief.   There can be no sound company-union relationship unless there is a sound foreman-steward understanding.

Increased efficiency through the foreman-steward relationship is illustrated by the experience of the Doehler-Jarvis Corporation.   The company, back in 1940, renewed its agreement with the CIO's Casting Division.   The contract called for a joint approach to improve plant efficiency. Company and union appointed representatives to plant production committees.   Each side chose only those people that were not involved in bargaining.   "Cooperation for efficiency" was instituted.

Although the committee functioned fairly well, it was soon discovered that the elaborate superstructure of production committees was a mistake.   These committees did not include the actual leadership of both management and union.   Without the participation of this leadership, major productivity advances could not be made.   Without this leadership, the worker at the machine could not be made production-conscious.

Union and management reexamined their objectives and procedures.   They decided that the problem of improving plant efficiency was a problem of improving departmental efficiency.   The foreman is the departmental production executive.   The steward is the departmental morale executive.   Any efficiency approach would have to be built around them.   Union and management further decided that productive efficiency could be obtained only by building an understanding and confidence in each worker that such efficiency "paid off." *Collective bargaining matures into cooperative planning.*

The Doehler-Jarvis Company and the union embarked upon a program of encouragement of conscious cooperation among foremen, stewards, and workers. These were the people who would determine the success of "cooperation for efficiency." Committee structures and suggestion mechanisms outside the mainstream of the daily union-management bargaining relationship are unnecessary. Plant manager and union executive board; superintendent and chief steward; foreman, steward, and worker —these are the channels for the teamwork approach to efficiency.

Labor-management production committees are formed outside regular union-management contact channels because management considers union relationship purely negative— arguments, grievances, restrictions. This management attitude will not harness the creative energies of thousands of workers. Labor-management committees are no substitutes for the creation of confidence in each worker that increasing productivity is the only way to a rising living standard. Such confidence is necessary if full worker participation is desired. That confidence can be built only by utilizing the worker's instrumentality, the union, as the mechanism for worker expression on efficiency advances.

The Doehler Company and the union, gravitating toward production with freedom, abolished their top labor-management committees in 1943. They established a permanent production committee in each department. It consists of every employee in the department and is headed by the foreman and steward. Production is not a once-in-a-while matter to be discussed monthly by committees. Production is an *every-minute* matter and is the concern of everyone.

Just before the end of the Second World War, the government addressed a questionnaire on production committees to various plants throughout the country. The Doehler Company replied that they had abolished their formal production committees and had achieved a cooperative approach to efficiency through the regular collective-bargaining channels.   The company stated:

> We have instructed our foremen that we feel the steward elected by the men in his department, should be taken into close confidence as regards the management of the department.   We feel that the steward should know certain schedules have to be met and that he should know everything that affects the department.

To move from collective bargaining to the higher level of union-management relations requires reeducating of the steward and the worker.   It also means reeducating the foreman.   Doehler foremen welcome worker ideas.   Gone is the old attitude, "You use your back; I'll do the thinking around here."   Foremen no longer feel that worker suggestions undermine their prestige.

A story is told of the preunion days in one of the Doehler plants.   A worker had the job of filing four projections from a flange.   This filing required exactly four strokes. The employee got the idea of welding two files together and completing the job in two strokes.   He was told by the foreman that it was impractical.   A few weeks later he discovered that management had introduced a double file, and he was further told that it was the result of the foreman's brainstorm.   That is a common experience in many plants.   As a result of such experience, workers hold back production ideas.   The new foreman-steward approach to production at Doehler's is eliminating the "mental sit-down."

The Doehler Company has become a national model for sound labor relations.   The secret of their success is the acceptance of "production with freedom" by company and union, foreman and steward, and each individual employee.

The successful use of the union-management relationship to obtain productive efficiency is illustrated by the CIO steelworkers and a Pittsburgh concern manufacturing water heaters.   The union and the company jointly explored the productive possibilities of the plant.   In 1937 the firm was producing an average of fifty-one heaters daily.   That production record by 1941 had been increased to sixty-five heaters.   The increase of 28 per cent resulted *solely* from the application of union-management cooperation for efficiency advances.   There was no addition of man power. Paralleling the production increase was an astonishing decrease in waste.   In 1937, prior to union-management efficiency talks, an average of four water heaters per day were returned for defective parts or faulty assembly.   At the end of 1940 only one such unit had been returned during the preceding fifteen months.

The efficiency record resulted in earnings for both company and worker.   The company recorded a loss of $50,000 in 1937.   In 1940 the profits were equal to the loss during 1937.   Employee earnings also rose.   The annual take-home pay in 1940 was 30 per cent higher than in 1937. Production and democracy applied to this plant paid dividends in cash and in sound, peaceful labor-management relations.

The Doehler Company, Westinghouse, Monsanto Chemical, and many other companies have proved the truth of Woodrow Wilson's statement: "The highest and best form of efficiency is the spontaneous cooperation of a free people."

The question that confronts America is not whether unions are here permanently.   That subject is academic. Unions have tripled their membership in the last decade. They will continue to grow.   The real question is, "What effect will unions have on our economy?   Will they be a negative force, confined to checks and restraints?   Or will they prove a positive force, acting for improved worker morale and increased production?"   The answer will determine the shape of things to come.   And the answer depends upon management and upon union.   America can accept nothing less than the maturing of collective bargaining to the higher stage of cooperative planning.

CHAPTER VI

HOW FAST IS FAST?

A Detroit foundry was experiencing a great deal of employee dissatisfaction. The disputes centered around incentive earnings and rates. The union maintained that the rates were low. The company argued that the rates were correct. Company-union discussions were leading nowhere. Finally, the company, disgusted with the bickering, eliminated the incentive. It had hoped that this would solve the problem. The abolition of the incentive solved nothing, for now the arguments centered on production pace and task. Again the company maintained that its production output assignment per hour was correct. The union argued that the assigned output per hour was too high. Both sides were bitter, suspicious, and adamant. That situation characterizes much of Detroit's industrial scene today.

By far the greatest single cause of unrest in industry today is to be found in the related issues of the rate of production, the required output per hour, and incentive rates. Involved in these issues is not only the question of industrial harmony but also the vital question of productivity. Unless this problem is solved there can be no hope for industrial peace and progress. The achievement of an agreement on what constitutes normal work output per man per hour is no easy matter. But it can be done. I contend that it is not fundamental difference that lies at the bottom of this conflict on output, task, and incentive rate, but rather lack of understanding and ignorance of modern methods of fair work measurement. Those methods—motion analysis and time study—are being used successfully in a good many companies. And in the understanding and proper application of these techniques lies the hope for a sound resolution of many present labor-management difficulties.

Labor's mistrust of scientific management in general has led to a fear of motion analysis and time study. Yet labor stands to benefit because the very purpose of these management tools is the elimination of worker fatigue. Our modern time-study department is not interested in strenuousness. The worker is simply asked to take advantage of better work arrangement. Strenuousness and efficiency are opposites. The easiest way is always the best way. The new time study has nothing in common with practices whereby increased production is sought by pushing the worker to greater effort instead of through better use of his time and energy. *The time-study department aims at conservation of human energy, not its excessive expenditure.*

The conservation of energy is illustrated by the work of Robert Carter, of the University of Vermont. Through an application of time-and-motion study to dairy chores he reduced the work time on a farm by two hours and five minutes a day. Travel on a farm was reduced by 730 miles per year.

The average worker, and many managements for that matter, are confused on this subject of time study. The subject still has to be "sold." Many believe that only those plants that have incentive-wage payments need have a time-study department. Others feel that where incentives do not exist, time-study departments are established to "drive" the worker. With or without incentives, with or without worker speed-up, every plant must have a time-study department.

The time standards developed by this department are essential for accurate pricing of the product. Industry uses accounting—cost standards—to compute overhead and material cost. It uses time standards in the computation of labor costs. Time standards are necessary for accurate production planning. With the knowledge of necessary job time, production can be scheduled. Equipment load and floor layout can be efficiently planned. Delivery dates can be safely predicted. Time study is an important instrumentality in the operation of the modern plant.

Whether time study is used for scheduling of production, pricing, cost, setting of production or, task, or as a basis for incentive payment, its primary function is *accurate work measurement*. The time-study engineer's objective is the ascertaining of the actual time required for an average operator to perform the job in the easiest and best manner. There are numerous methods and theories regarding the most accurate method of work measurement. But the purpose of time-study technique is to give management an accurate and consistent time yardstick.

Battleships, concrete mixers, bobby pins, battery boxes— they all take *time* to build. Measurement of time is important to industry. It is also important to labor. Labor power per unit of *time* is the one thing the worker has to sell. The manufacturer pays the worker for his energy expenditure in a given time interval. If the worker does not produce, the employer does not get the value he should for the wages he pays. On the other hand, if the employee works harder or faster than "normal" he does not receive full payment for his time—unless he is paid for the extra work above the "normal" through some sort of an incentive-pay plan.

Both worker and manager, therefore, are vitally interested in this matter of work measurement. They must both be desirous of establishing a fair day's work. They must determine exactly how much time it should take a "normal" or "average" experienced employee working at an "average" or "normal" pace to perform certain operations under a given set of conditions.

A "fair day's work" yardstick has been established for many motions. Walking is one example. Three miles per hour is the average speed of a man walking on a flat, horizontal surface and carrying nothing. This three-miles-per-hour figure is obtained from actual tests of thousands of walkers. This "normal" speed can be maintained by the average walker without undue fatigue.

Typing is another common operation about which there has been a great deal of quantitative study. The speed of of the average office typist is fifty-seven words a minute. This speed is considered "normal."

In walking and typing we are able to get accurate work measurement. We can establish an average performance. We record the time of thousands of walkers who are asked to walk normally. By assembling these data and applying proved mathematical formulas for "normal distribution" we arrive at an average or normal figure. Thus we get the normal walking performance. Against this normal-performance yardstick we can measure accurately the slow and the fast walker. After all, "fast" and "slow" are only relative terms. A person is fast or slow in terms of the average.

Time-study men must be limited solely to work measurement. Their language is one of *time*. The time-study department's goal must be development of standards of normal work, of average performance. This is not the performance of a superman or a slow man, a young man or an old man. It is not the killing pace or the waste-of-time pace. It is the performance that an average man can be expected to maintain the entire day. It is a pace that reflects conscientious effort. It is to the job what three miles per hour is to walking.

The achievement of accurate work measurement is a task for both management and labor. The understanding of its *function* is also of prime importance. That the part played by work measurement is not fully grasped is evidenced by the AFL slogan of a "fair day's pay for a fair day's work." The AFL has for over fifty years associated fair payment and normal work. There is no relevance between a fair wage and a fair day's work. Wages may vary with economic conditions, union organization, type of industry, plant profit situation, cost of living, and other similar factors. National productivity may increase wages and what wages will buy. The unit of work, however, should go on indefinitely in the same sense as any other standard measurement. Management and labor must understand the role of work measurement. Normal work standards and wage payment must be separated.

The confusion of the concepts of standards and payment can be seen if applied to the purchase of a farm. If seller and buyer should bargain on price per acre, with both having different concepts of acre size, there could be no agreement. Price may fluctuate but an acre remains an acre. Imagine the chaos if each individual had his own idea of how much land an acre should encompass. Trade is impossible without standards of measurement. The same thing must be applied to industry. At the present time, labor and management are bargaining on price and "acre size." There is resultant chaos. Work measurement, with the establishment of normal work standards, will eliminate argument on the "size of an acre." All sections of the industrial world need to talk the same language if they want to settle differences.

The separation of time from money and the establishment of the normal-work yardstick is the key to successful operation of incentive plans and the setting of proper production output. It is also the key to the resolution of 90 per cent of union-management disputes in the plant. There may be arguments on earnings, rates, or output, but underlying these debates is hidden the fundamental disagreement of what constitutes normal work. Or, how fast *is* fast? Many times management and labor are unconscious of this basic difference on normal performance. They continue heated debates over long periods of time without realizing that they are not talking the same language. They use the same words but the words carry different meanings to each side. They never realize that their disagreement lies in basic concepts and not in the particular end result in dispute.

Take the problem of setting an incentive rate. There are four basic factors involved:

1. The fixed hourly wage
2. The time allowances for fatigue and delay
3. The actual time recorded for the job
4. The normalizing or leveling factor

The first three factors are fixed and definite. The hourly wage is fixed by contract. Time allowances on the job are stipulated. The actual time for the performance of the operation is read from a stop watch. Those three items, therefore, are easily computed and checked. Union-management agreement on these points is readily obtained and is based on facts. It is the fourth factor—normalizing —that underlies labor-management quarrels.

This normalizing factor—or effort rating—is used in the time study to correct, either up or down, the actual recorded time in which the job is performed. This connection is necessary because the hourly wage paid is keyed to an average performance. The time-study objective is finding the normal time for the particular job. Since it is not practical to seek an "average operator" every time a time study is made, the time-study engineer normalizes his study. He *judges* whether the operator exceeded or dropped below normal performance. He then adjusts his recorded time. This normalizing is an attempt at accurate work measurement.

There is the case of a die-casting company in Toledo. It had always experienced good labor relations. The company, however, was finding this question of incentive rates very troublesome. Numerous heated debates were taking place. Company and union, although arguing monetary rates, were actually in dispute on time rates. To prove this to both parties, the union's national chairman, who had been called into the situation, suggested that the four union stewards and the four company time study men go out into the shop and spend a day speed-rating the workers. Both sides accepted. No watches were used. Each person judged the operator's performance and recorded it. The ratings were kept secret until the project was completed. At the end of the day the ratings were tabulated. The results showed that on the average the company men had rated worker performance at 140 per cent, that is, 40 per cent above normal. The union representatives had rated worker performance at 160 per cent. Company and union differed by 20 points on their concept of normal performance.

When this fact was brought to light, the company and the union proceeded to discuss the definition of "normal work." With the aid of a consulting engineering firm, an agreement on the concept of "normal" was arrived at. Both sides are now working from the same definitions. Debate will take place in the same language. They have separated "fair payment" from "fair work." If the men desire greater earnings they will proceed to bargain for an increased hourly wage. If the company feels its labor costs are high and desire to reduce them, it will bargain for a reduced hourly wage. In neither case will the work standard be touched.

Accurate work measurement will benefit labor in many ways. Besides serving as a sound basis for incentive payment, it will end individual foreman judgment of worker efficiency. "Riding" the individual by supervision for greater output will disappear. Definite standards of output will be determined systematically and every worker will meet regular schedules, not a foreman's concept of a "fair day's work."

Time study and work measurement are here to stay. They cannot be eliminated by any worker movement. They are an integral part of the factory system. The union that opposes time study is assuming the impractical role of those early weavers that smashed the spinning machines. The intelligent unionist will attempt to understand time study and perfect its application so that labor and management may receive the full benefits from this modern-management instrument.

The perfection, not the abolition, of time study must be labor's position. Time-study methods, at present, are far from precise. There is too much "art" and not enough "science" in the determination of normal standards of performance. This condition is due to the presence of human judgment in the estimate of operator efficiency and pace during time studies. As long as work measurement depends upon this subjective approach, error is bound to appear.

Time-study experts themselves, are the first to point out that time study is a technique and not a science. Ralph Presgrave, management representative, and author of the *Dynamics of Time Study*, takes great pains to point out the inadequacies of this management tool. On numerous occasions he has stated:

> I do not think anyone will accuse me of dragging a skeleton out of the closet if I say that time study has fallen considerably in the estimate of a great many people. I think the blame can be laid at our doors. We have made, or have permitted to be made, errors that have led us into quite a number of difficulties. I think most of these errors were honest and probably not intentional and, because of the developing stage of the profession, with meager information to go on, were probably unavoidable.
>
> Criticism has been mostly on the emotional side. If the criticism had been objective and had been made by people with technical knowledge, I am not too sure that time study would have survived. *Now, however, I think we have knowledge and experience and information*

*enough to enable us to cleanse the profession of many of
these faults.*

Let's admit it. Time study in its present stage of
development is only quasi measurement. Actually it is a
form of relative grading of worker effort because the
necessary measuring tools for precise measurement are not
yet available. But time study is our best present technique
for work measurement.

Without a speedometer, trained individuals might guess
automobile speed fairly accurately. But the speedometer
removes from the realm of debate the determination of
automobile speed. The problem of establishing standard
work measurement is not as simple as constructing a
speedometer. In the former case we deal with a man and
all of his complex motions. Developing standards for
normal time of motions involves great problems. There are
the motions of various members of the body. These
motions may be restricted or unrestricted. One company
alone, the Murray Corporation, in time-studying its jobs
has catalogued some 300,000 elemental motions. Over a
five-year period it has developed "standard-time" for these
different motions.

There are many groups working on this problem.
Industrial engineers are attempting to minimize and eventually eliminate human judgment in effort rating. They
hope to achieve the mechanical precision of an "effort meter"
so that worker speed may be accurately determined and
normal work standards set. Some universities are conduct-
ing research on this problem of scientific work measurement.
They are testing present methods in their laboratories.
Their work will help develop the techniques and technology
that will yield the precise time yardstick.

The Society for the Advancement of Management is also
working on this problem. It has established a Committee
on Rating of Time Studies, with the hope of providing coordi-
nated study of the problem on a national basis. The com-

mittee recognizes the need for improvement in time-study methods. It is endeavoring to establish national rating standards and thus put work measurement, if not on a scientific basis, at least on a systematized and consistent basis.

This rating committee has two principle objectives. It wants to improve the quality of rating as presently practiced. It advocates the substitution of individual judgment in time studies by group judgment. Judgment error is narrowed by group rating. Normal-work concepts are discussed by groups in the training period. Where unions participate, both company and union representatives attend the same training classes and receive the same instruction in normal rating.

Ultimately, however, the committee hopes to find a more concrete and superior solution. Objective measurements with instruments are the best answer. The development of these instruments will come. Human judgment is only an intermediate step. The microscope transformed medicine from a craft to a science. Precision tools for work measurement will do the same for time study.

Constructive collective bargaining is the successful approach to this most complex of factory problems—work measurement. Management sits down with the union committee and discusses its plans for work measurement. Perhaps an impartial industrial engineer has been invited by both sides to attend and guide the discussion. Management outlines the rules and program for work measurement as they are to be applied to the plant. Everyone participates in the discussion. Fundamental concepts are explored. Opinions are exchanged on what constitutes normal performance. The methods for measuring normal work are questioned. The meeting develops into an excellent round-table discussion on time-and-motion study—its functions, advantages, and limitations. Out of this discussion, with its exchange of management and worker *experience* and *outlook*, comes a fundamental agreement on *work-measurement policy*.

The agreed-upon policy is then submitted for discussion and vote to the workers in the plant. The submission of this work-measurement policy entails worker education. Meetings are held and questions asked and answered. Well-illustrated booklets, written in simple language, are distributed. The worker for the first time learns about normal performance, work measurement, and time-study methods. He discovers why the separation of time and money are necessary. He learns the function of the time-study steward. He begins to understand time-study language and its purpose.

The worker's vote of approval of the work-measurement policy carries with it his confidence in fair time study. That confidence flows from his new understanding. Time-study procedures, as outlined in the adopted policy, become part of the factory law.

The adoption of the work-measurement policy does not alter management's rights and responsibilities. As in the past, production standards are determined by management. Management is responsible for the administration of time study. The union does not assume any management function. It does continue its policing function. In order properly to check administration of work measurement, the union elects time-study stewards. These time-study stewards are trained in the techniques of work measurement. They are the union's "time auditors." They act only when the worker complains that the company has violated the established work-measurement policy.

Management, in some cases, may not be willing to permit union participation in the determination of work-measurement policy. It may feel that such participation is an undermining of management prerogative. Management may argue that union participation on the policy level would lead to an impossible situation if agreement would not be reached on the concept of normal performance.

But management cannot sidestep a discussion of work measurement and normal performance. Refusing union participation in policy making merely shifts the scene of debate. Instead of a calm discussion, based upon facts, in the conference room, management gets hundreds of individual arguments, day after day, down in the shop. For management it is not a question of argument or no argument. Rather it is a question of where and when the discussion takes place. All the advantages are with the procedure of union participation in policy making.

The management that is reluctant to permit union participation in time study should note that work measurement still involves some human judgment. Wherever human judgment exists there is an area of possible disagreement. This disagreement cannot be resolved by standing on one's prerogatives. In a democracy disagreements are resolved through discussion and understanding. Understanding results from an exchange of viewpoints. This applies to the concept of normal performance. If there were in existence precision work-measurement tools, the determination of work-measurement policy would be relatively simple. In the absence of these tools, management, if it desires productivity and harmony, must submit its judgment of work measurement to the test of union-management discussion.

Union participation in time study democratizes "scientific" management. This democratization creates worker confidence in technical-management tools. First, it lets the worker know what time study really is. Second, it keeps him informed on how it is being applied by management, and finally, it gives him the right to check the application through his own trained representative.

The Murray Corporation of Detroit and its CIO local have pioneered in the joint approach to work measurement. This company hired an industrial engineering firm that trained in the art of work measurement five elected union time-study stewards. Union men attended classes with company time-study men for a period of six months. Now all "time" grievances are routed to the union time-study stewards. The program has been eminently successful.

In four years not a single grievance on time study has had to be arbitrated. All of them have been settled by discussion between company and union time-study representatives. Further proof of the program's success has been the reelection, without opposition, of all of the union time-study stewards.

Edmund P. Dylenski, one of the union time-study stewards, explains his function:

The union steward does not make any original studies used for establishing production standards. The time study-steward enters the picture only when a grievance is brought to him. Perhaps the time study is satisfactory and the trouble is due to methods; in that case the cause of the difficulty is pointed out to the foreman. If we believe that the standards are inaccurate, we talk the matter over with the company time-study engineer. We always settle the case.

Other companies and unions are developing a joint approach to the work-measurement problem. In all instances good results are reported. The Packard Company, employing some 40,000 people, has had twenty-six men and women trained in time study by an outside engineering firm. Thirteen of those trainees are CIO union representatives.

George T. Christopher, Packard president, in introducing the union-management program, wrote: "Both the company and the workers want . . . fair measurement of a day's work. With everybody striving towards that end, the project becomes another evidence of how company and union, working together, can achieve a further advance in the common cause."

Management has the responsibility for selling time study and its uses. Not only worker and steward, but also foreman and supervisor should understand how time study is used and how it is not. Management has still another responsibility. It must democratize and humanize time study. This can be accomplished by accepting and training the union time-study steward.

The participation of the union in work measurement provides the foundation for ascertaining proper production output. Accurate and consistent work measurement eliminates the issue of productivity from the sphere of emotions and prejudices. It is fundamental to insuring industrial harmony. It is the practical application of production with freedom to the daily problems of factory management. Without sound work measurement, collective bargaining cannot succeed.

CHAPTER VII

PRIVATE ENTERPRISE ON THE JOB!

The incentive wage is the greatest single stimulant to increased output per labor-hour. Union endorsement of productivity necessitates the acceptance of incentives. There is no side-stepping this fact. The joint approach for efficiency advances, whether through the foreman-steward relationship or the labor-management production committee, can accomplish much. It is not, however, a substitute for the incentive program.

The incentive wage, because it is a method of payment designated to compensate the worker in relation to his productivity, increases PMH. The incentive develops individual initiative. It is private enterprise on the job. It puts every worker into business for himself. The incentive benefits everyone—more wages for the worker, more production and lower costs for the industrialist, and more goods at lower prices for the consumer.

Incentive-wage plans are no cure-all for our industrial ills. They are *not* intended to replace the necessary and constant improvement in product design, scheduling, supervision, and factory planning. These are essential if we are to achieve an ever-increasing industrial output. The incentive, however, is the most practical way of getting more from our existing man power, factory, and equipment because it rewards the individual, immediately and directly, for better use of his time and effort.

This monetary reward is important to the worker. The most recent wage figures of the Department of Labor show that average earnings in manufacturing plants amount to about $42 for a full work week. The average worker is very much interested in the possibility of increasing his earnings $12 or $15 per week. He *can* do this by increasing his output.   During the war period the War Labor Board kept complete records on earnings in those plants where incentives were instituted.   Their files show that the incentive worker earns one third more than the hourly rated worker in the same time at the same job.

The war experience has proved the relation of incentives and increased production.   Increases in man-hour output, after the introduction of incentive payments, have been phenomenal.   Reports by management to the War Labor Board on the operation of new wage-incentive plans during 1944 indicate that, on the average, an increase in production per man-hour of about 40 per cent occurred in the first ninety days of incentive operation.   These reports covered one million workers.   This production increase was matched by a 15 to 20 per cent increase in earnings and a 10 to 15 per cent *decrease* in unit cost of product.

The American Management Association also conducted a survey on incentive results.   Its questionnaire went out to representative firms from coast to coast.   The response corroborated the WLB record.   In each instance where the company had changed from hourly payment to an incentive wage, man-hour production was increased from 20 to 50 per cent.   Many of the machining operations that were changed from payment by the hour to payment by results showed over 50 per cent increase in output.

This record of increased production is not due solely to increased physical effort by the worker.   In most cases, the application of payment by result led to more efficient work methods.   It inspired each individual in labor and management to think and work up to his capacity.   One of the most important advantages of incentives is the pressure it puts on management to do its part in getting more production.   Management must review work methods. It must find the best way to do the job.   It must plan and schedule to provide a continuous flow of material to the operator at the machine.   The establishment of the incentive places upon management the responsibility for keeping nonproductive time to a minimum. Unless this is done, no bonus is earned and there is worker dissatisfaction. This worker pressure for efficient supervision has been no small factor in the achievement of production increases.

W. E. Eargle, of the Westinghouse Corporation, recently illustrated the relationship of incentives and efficiency from his own company's experience. Westinghouse, among other things, manufactures thick concrete slabs that are used for factory-roof construction. The installation of a proper incentive plan entailed a job study with its resultant work simplification. Prior to the job analysis, production totaled 80 slabs daily. The establishment of the incentive plan, with its better work methods, increased production to 425 slabs daily. Production, with the same crew, rose almost 400 per cent. Each man's earnings were nearly doubled. In spite of rising earnings unit cost was cut almost in half—a result of reduced overhead costs.

All this was accomplished without "taking it out of the hide of the worker." The company analyzed the operations. It instituted the simplest and easiest motion routine. Based upon this routine it established a fair day's work. It then installed payment by result. The incentive created worker interest and cooperation in greater output.

Incentive pay can be used to improve not only quantity but also quality of product. During the Second World War Lyon Incorporated of Detroit made cartridge cases and shells. It also necessarily made scrap, which it did not want. It offered incentive pay for less scrap. That is, it offered more pay for better work. It reduced its production of scrap on automatic machine operations by more than 90 per cent. Lyons reported that after the installation of the incentive, its plant produced 25 per cent more than normal at a considerably reduced cost per unit.

Practical proof of the advantages of incentives is the experience of the Lincoln Electric Manufacturing Company of Cleveland. This company makes one half of the country's and one quarter of the world's electric-welding machines and supplies. It has built its sales on quality but also on low prices. In the last twenty-six years it has reduced the price of a typical welding machine from $1500 to $200. In the last twelve years it has reduced the price of a typical electrode—a steel rod with a chemical coating—from fifteen cents a pound to a little over five cents.

Lincoln is the world's low-cost welding producer. It is also the world's highest factory-wage payer. Lincoln believes that no wage is too high if it is earned. In prewar 1941 its workers averaged some $4800 a year. This works out at about $2 per hour per worker, well over *twice* the average factory wage. How is it done? It is done utterly by an *incentive* that produces *unity of effort* by the management and the worker. Lincoln calls it "incentive management."

One would think that the increased production and earnings offered by incentive-wage plans would make such plans generally accepted. The contrary is true. In spite of the advantages of incentives, less than one third of America's workers are presently covered. Here is a tremendous potential for productivity increase. Two-thirds of our labor force could better its man-hour output 20 to 50 per cent. Just as important, this group of Americans could increase substantially its purchasing power while reducing unit production cost. Here, for the picking, are America's "acres of diamonds."

Incentives have not been widely applied because they have been misunderstood and feared. Management's fear of incentives is based upon the belief that high earnings will become a new standard for an hourly wage without the maintenance of corresponding high production. It feels that incentives lead to *inflated* earnings and eventual collapse of the entire wage structure. Labor, on the other hand, fears rate cutting. The worker has experienced the use of incentives to get more and more work for the same or even less pay. Labor feels that incentives lead to *deflated* earnings and the eventual undermining of its wage positions.

While management fears only inflated earnings and labor fears only deflated earnings, both inflation and deflation should worry both. It is characteristic of any successful incentive plan that it must operate fairly. The incentive plan that is not a good proposition for each side is not a good proposition for either.

Labor's fear, however, is the major obstacle to the introduction of incentives. Workers reject incentives "on principle." They associate incentives with scientific management. Worker opposition to scientific management dates from the early days of Frederick W. Taylor, one of America's early efficiency engineers. Workingmen have resented the very term "scientific management" because they have felt that it is the antithesis of human management. Labor has identified scientific management with dictatorial management practices. Efficiency experts have abused and misused management's efficiency tools. The worker now feels, as a result of those experiences, that efficiency is the turning of man into a machine. To the overwhelming majority of America's wage earners incentives and scientific management have meant this:

Management sends a time-study man to observe a worker at his machine. The observer has a watch that divides a minute not merely into sixty parts but into a hundred. With its help he records the exact length of time required for a certain operation. Management offers the worker so many cents per operation.

So the worker gets to work. He "speeds up." He cuts the required time for the operation. He climbs, let us say, to $1.50 an hour. Management then uses this new production record as the basic required time for the operation and sets a new rate. The worker now earns no more going fast than he used to earn going slow.

This has happened to millions of workers in American industry. It makes workers wary. It makes them hold back. Yet this practice bears as little resemblance to modern, sound, incentive plans as the oxcart does to the airplane.

It is this practice, however, that has led to the situation where the CIO's United Auto Workers, the world's largest union, opposes the introduction of incentive-pay plans. The 1943 convention of this union, of over one million members, instructed its officers, staff, and local unions to "conform strictly to union policy on incentives." What is this policy?

UAW-CIO reiterates emphatically its traditional opposition to the introduction of incentives or piece-work plans in the plants within our jurisdiction.

The resolution opposing incentives stated that such action was necessary because incentives "aggravated the dislocation and unbalancing of production schedules, resulting in layoffs and unemployment." And further, "incentives would reintroduce the old system of speed-up, in which the worker is robbed of higher earnings through management's use of every insignificant engineering change or pretext to cut rates."

The UAW resolution reflects the sentiment of a majority of its membership. It was reaffirmed at a meeting of the International Board in April, 1946. The resolution charges that increased productivity will lead to unemployment, and further, such productivity will lead to more and more work for the same wage payment. The first charge has been exploded in the opening chapters of this book. *Productivity leads to jobs.* The second charge, that of "speed-up," is not new. It is, also, not true. Incentive opponents have long said, "Incentives with their speed-up drives the worker at breakneck speed. In a few years the man is a physical and nervous wreck. He is burnt out." This is a confusion of work-at-capacity and speed-up. Modern incentives have nothing in common with speed-up. They ask only conscientious application by the worker to his job.

Labor's acceptance of incentives underwrites its acceptance of productivity. It also establishes a community of interest with management that develops sound industrial relations. General Motors is the UAW's biggest customer. If UAW desires constructive labor-management relations in the automobile industry, it must achieve it with General Motors. The union's position on incentives is not only unsound from a productivity standpoint, but also unsound in that it contributes to an irreconcilable conflict with General Motors. General Motors maintains that it wants production. It has requested the UAW to "withdraw its opposition and lend its support to individual piece-work or other incentive methods of pay." It has pointed out to union officials that the "corporation is satisfied that the introduction of incentive pay will increase production from 10 per cent to 25 per cent without increase of man power." UAW, if it desires to practice production plus democracy will have to rescind its opposition to incentive-pay plans.

The UAW and other unions will have to revise their position on incentive plans. They can accept incentives and protect the health and earnings of their membership through certain safeguards. These safeguards will prevent the abuses that have occurred in the past. They will put incentives on a sound basis—acceptable to everyone. No one can deny that the stop watch, the slide rule, the motion camera have been used by some managements as speed-up and stretch-out devices. That still occurs. It is, however, less and less frequent. Modern incentives are based upon modern time study. Time-and-motion study today stimulates increased production through the introduction of *best work methods*. Union endorsement of, and participation in, time study can help advance the *proper* use of the incentive principle.

Labor has charged that incentives result in uncertain earnings. Labor can demand that the incentive is not substituted for a "real" wage. Incentives *supplement* the regular wage and *do not* take its place. The guaranteed hourly earnings under any incentive-wage system must at least equal the hourly wage rate that would be paid if there were no incentive plan in effect.

Labor has maintained that it does not benefit from increased production to the extent that management does. Unions should insist on full participation in the results from increased production. Extra payment for extra effort should be on a 100 per cent basis. If two hours of work are done in one, then two hours pay should be the reward for that one hour of work. Full participation in benefits from increased production requires that hourly output be rewarded on an hourly basis and not averaged out for the day. Performance on the job for part of the day should not be averaged against performance on another job for the rest of the day. Unions can demand that special allowances be paid for unmeasured work such as samples, untimed jobs, and salvage. Finally, rate cutting can be eliminated by an agreement that no time standard be changed once it is determined, unless there is an appreciable change in work content.

There is still another reason for the maximum use of incentives. During the war a good many unions endorsed incentives because they were in agreement upon the necessity for more and more production. The need for production has not ceased. The devastation of war, plus the unbelievably low living standards of millions of people throughout the world, demands ever increasing productivity in America.

American labor and management must practice productivity not only for their own sakes, but also for the sake of the world and its future. Our worker, our manager, can best contribute to world peace by producing tremendous quantities of needed goods. While governments of all nations must arrange for a smooth flow of these goods, there will be no purpose in international political and economic collaboration unless labor and management here produce in abundance. The acceptance of incentives can help achieve high-level production.

Along with accepting high-level production, America, to do its part in the building of a peaceful world, must adopt new concepts of foreign trade. Selling abroad has always had the support of business and labor. That half of foreign trade was enthusiastically endorsed. The other half, that of buying from abroad, has not been so warmly received. It is encouraging to note, however, that there is a swing toward accepting the fundamental truth that foreign trade consists of imports as well as exports. Selling without buying is not trade; it is economic warfare and can result only in another world conflagration.

The American Bankers Association, the U. S. Chamber of Commerce, the National Association of Manufacturers, the Committee for Economic Development, the CIO and the AFL have all announced support of "two-way foreign trade." That industry and labor support expanding import is good news. With their cooperation the government can move to eradicate our barriers to imports.

The removal of our barriers to imports can in some cases be facilitated by the acceptance of incentives. It is not a long pull from *opposition* to that excellent stimulant to increased production, the incentive wage, to the *advocacy* of high tariffs. Labor at a certain zinc-smelting plant in Illinois has opposed the introduction of an incentive-wage plan. Labor at that plant has also been opposed to any reduction of our tariff on imported zinc. Incentives, with its rationalization of work methods, could increase the PMH of this particular smelter by over 100 per cent. It would put the smelter on a "competitive" basis with foreign zinc. Labor, no longer threatened with job loss, would in this instance, withdraw its support of economic isolation. The acceptance of productivity techniques by the Union at this Illinois smelter would strengthen the cause of world trade.

Effective international cooperation will require intelligent government action on tariff policy, cartels, commodity agreements, monetary stability, international loans and credits, and other programs devised to stimulate world commerce. Such action is necessary for it is now perfectly clear that the United States cannot live in isolation— military, political, or economic. Our economic health will affect other nations; theirs will affect us. Foreign and domestic policy are two sides of the same coin. Our domestic policy of abundance will breed the same policy abroad. Depression and unemployment abroad will develop it here. The world-wide economic crisis of the nineteen thirties proved that. The antidote for the paralyzing poison of world depression is ever-expanding world trade and economic cooperation. And that means the full utilization of *all* of our productive resources. That should include the technique of incentive-wage plans.

A general educational program on the advantages of incentive wage payments is a necessity. This program must reach the public and government as well as management and labor. There is too much national misunderstanding of this vital subject. This nation cannot afford to lose the productivity resulting from incentives merely because there is a lack of popular knowledge of this subject. Everyone must become familiar with the benefits of work simplification, motion economy, and extra payment for extra effort. These are the foundations of the incentive program. They point the way to greater and greater productivity increases, and an ever-increasing living standard here and abroad. They also serve as a strong foundation for industrial harmony.

CHAPTER VIII

WHAT'S A MAN WORTH?

Production is not solely a matter of technology and machines. It also involves human factors. Worker attitudes are reflected in production efficiency. Employee dissatisfaction creates an environment in which no productivity technique can flourish. Union-management efforts for efficiency advances, whether through the joint production committee, the suggestion system, or the incentive wage, are dependent for success upon the "frame of mind" of the individual. High worker morale is essential for high PMH. The greatest single factor in achieving this high worker morale is a *sound wage policy*. It is also another essential for sound collective bargaining.

Sound wage policy is more than just adequate wage payment. It is wage payment based upon the individual's contribution to the success of the enterprise. It is wage payment based upon the *kind* of job done and the *efficiency* with which it is done. It is reward for services rendered, not only through wage payment, but also through opportunity for job promotion. Sound wage policy is the embodiment of the principle of *individuality in industry*.

This principle of individuality—full recognition of individual differences in skill and effort—is the fundamental theme of sound wage policy. The creation of a wage structure that reflects that policy is a formidable task. But unless such a wage structure is established, employee dissatisfaction results. In such a situation the best-laid plans for productivity expansion cannot succeed.

Management has not given the matter of wage principles the attention it deserves. As a result, policy on wage and promotion matters is nonexistent in many companies. Their wage structures have "just growed." A sweeper who works in one plant for a number of years may eventually, through length-of-service increases, receive the rate being paid a tool-and-die maker. A machine operator transferred from one job to another, without rate adjustment when the transfer occurs, may be receiving twenty cents more per hour than the worker next to him doing the same job. The absence of standard hiring rates may establish wage inequalities that endure for years and years. Favoritism in disbursing individual wage increases creates differentials. Even where favoritism is not present, the practice of allowing the foreman or supervisor arbitrarily to judge the worth of a job, or the value of an individual, has led to a conglomeration of random rates. Sound wage policy demands that capricious wage setting end, and that systematic wage determination begin.

Systematic wage determination depends first upon the establishment of occupational relationships. The management that paid *all* of its employees two dollars an hour would soon discover that it lacked policy. Regardless of the amount paid, the skilled worker will not tolerate a wage structure that pays him exactly the same amount as the production worker. In turn, the semiskilled production worker would not long be happy with his two dollars per hour if the unskilled sweeper received a like sum. There are differences in the worth of jobs. The doctor and the plumber are not paid alike for services rendered. A proper relationship of job worth is necessary for workshop harmony. The occupational ladder, which lists all jobs from the sweeper at the bottom to the tool maker at the top, is a principled guide to differential wage payment based upon society's requirements for labor. The modern technique for ascertaining job relationships is job evaluation. It is an essential tool for developing sound wage policy.

Unfortunately, there is worker opposition to job evaluation. This opposition is based upon labor's general mistrust of "scientific" management techniques. It is also the result of an unfounded fear that job evaluation will be used to "mechanize" the worker. Labor's attitude is expressed in the reactions of some union officials. "Go ahead with your evaluation. We don't want to participate. Just tell us what comes out at the end. How much money for what job?" This attitude of "know-nothing" leads to intense argument. It substitutes emotion for fact as the basis for discussion. One cannot debate job rates intelligently if one does not know how the job relationship was derived. The "know-nothings" in labor's ranks do not contribute to harmonious, constructive union-management relations.

A Massachusetts manufacturer of plastics decided to eliminate from his plant the wage inequity—the invisible industrial "agitator." Management drew up a plan for replacing its chaotic wage structure. It called in its union committee and announced that it was going to institute a job-evaluation program as the first step in the establishment of a sound wage policy. After some explanation of the proposed plan, the plant manager inquired "Does the program meet with your approval?" The union committee chairman hesitated and then said, "No—and what's more, the rank and file are opposed to evaluation."

Management had not anticipated such a reaction. It had expected hearty union approval. For some time the union had been expressing dissatisfaction with the company's wage structure. It had presented numerous demands for wage increases for specific departments, jobs, and individuals. The union claimed that workers doing equal work received unequal pay. These wage differentials were a source of constant irritation. Any increase granted to an individual or a department was instantly met by a new flood of wage demands based upon new inequities created by the increase. It soon became apparent to management that only a new, rational wage structure based upon an occupational ladder could solve its wage problem and bring peace to its plant. Yet here was the union opposing the very thing it should have been supporting.

The plant manager, after some thought, turned to the union committee. "So you don't like evaluation. Let me ask you this. Do you fellows think we ought to pay a machine-hand and a porter the same wage?"

"Of course not," was the quick and unanimous reply.

"Well, you men have just conducted an evaluation of those two jobs. Even if you had replied 'yes' you would have evaluated them. Your answer meant that you were determining the relative worth of the occupations of machine-hand and porter. And that is the essence of evaluation. Now the company is proposing that we determine 'scientifically' the relative worth of all jobs in this plant."

This discussion was the beginning of the dissipation of union fears. Other talks followed. With understanding, came acceptance. The job evaluation program was a complete success.

The primary objective of job evaluation is the measurement of job relationships. Job evaluation does *not* concern itself with wage payment. In this respect it is similar to time study, where work measurement, not wage payment is the goal. In time study *work* measurement is obtained by the use of a yardstick—normal time to perform an operation. In job evaluation *job* measurement is achieved by the use of another yardstick—the factors that are common to all jobs.

Study men's occupations. They are composed of the same basic factors. These basic factors are present in all jobs, but they are present in varying degrees. Physical labor is present in the occupations of both ditch digging and lathe operating. Skill is also present in both jobs. These factors, however, are present in different degrees in each of the jobs. The degrees of *physical effort, skill, experience, responsibility, working conditions,* and other job factors serve as the graduations on the job yard-stick. The degrees of job factors present determine the relative job worth. Thus, a permanent yardstick is established to measure job value and construct the occupational ladder.

The proper application of the job yardstick is dependent on accurate job description. The job description details the facts, functions, and conditions of the particular job. It is a permanent record of job duties and characteristics. Should the content of the job change, the yardstick is applied to determine the job's new position on the occupational ladder. Should a new job be created the same yardstick appraises and places it on the proper rung of the ladder. Consistency of job relationships is thus constantly maintained.

A rational wage structure, embodying individuality in industry, is founded on accurate job evaluation. Union participation in the evaluation procedure is necessary if the results are wholeheartedly to be accepted. The worker will not accept the facts of job relationships if he has no confidence in the job measurement program. If management desires worker confidence in managerial techniques it will have to invite union consultation and participation.

P. W. Jones, Employee Relations Director of the Sperry Gyroscope Company, in 1937 developed, directed, and administered the first union-management evaluation program in the country. He said "The joint approach to evaluation eliminates the fight attitude."

The Sperry Gyroscope Company applied the principles of production with freedom to its problem of establishing a satisfactory wage structure. The union was invited to sit down and discuss the company's plans for accurate job measurement. Management outlined its program and asked for comment and criticism. Everyone participated in the discussion. The fundamental question of job yardstick was explored. Opinions, based upon the respective viewpoints and experiences, were exchanged. From that meeting, and others like it, came agreement on the evaluation program.

Sperry and other companies have realized that the creation of a job yardstick must come from democratic discussion if the stigma of arbitrariness is to be avoided. Job evaluation is not mathematically exact. It is a technique of systematic method by which *group judgment* analyzes job content and relative job worth. Because job evaluation is dependent upon human judgment, it is important that differences be ironed out at the judgment level. Sperry Gyroscope's recognition of this important point led to inviting the union to participate in yardstick creation. The joint approach to job evaluation did not curtail management's prerogatives. Here, as in every other management technique affecting labor, union participation was in policy making, not in administration. Management continued to do the managing.

Some of the worker opposition to job evaluation is based on the mistaken belief that job evaluation is an appraisal of the individual. This is a confusion between job-rating and man rating. Job measurement is interested in only job content and characteristics. It is not concerned with individual evaluation. The fact that a punch-press operator is college trained or especially proficient does not influence the grading of the punch-press occupation. The job requirements, not the individual's attributes or performance determine job value. Job evaluation itself is not concerned with individual performance or worth.

Individuality in industry, however, does call for measurement of individual performance. Payment based upon the *kind* of job done is ascertained from job measurement. A further refinement is necessary. Payment must also be based upon the efficiency with which the particular job is done. Unless both occupational differences and individual differences within the occupation are recognized, the basic principle of individuality is negated. Most unions and managements will agree that it is desirable to reward individual performance: management because it desires the increased productivity that results from improved individual performance; the union because it wants as much money as it can get for the worker. In spite of this seeming mutuality of interest in monetary reward for individual skill and effort, there is a wide divergence of positions on this issue. The result is that in many industries, payment on the individuality principle has been abolished.

The AFL building trades unions are advocates of the single-rate wage payment. Bill Smith, bricklayer, receives $1.75 an hour regardless of his output. Another bricklayer who turns in only 80 per cent of Smith's performance gets the same pay. In some plants there is a variation of the single rate, known as the bracket wage payment. Thus, the minimum rate for a tool maker may be $1.40 an hour and the maximum rate $1.60. Between this minimum and maximum there is a twenty-cent spread that ostensibly rewards individual performance. CIO unions in these plants, however, have requested the automatic length-of-service increase. The tool maker starting at $1.40 receives a five-cent increase at regular intervals until he reaches the top rate of $1.60. Eventually every tool maker receives the same rate. While individuality has been recognized to the extent that the tool maker does not receive the same wage rate as the sweeper, it has been denied to the extent that every tool maker, regardless of skill and effort, receives the same wage payment.

Management is generally opposed to the elimination of individuality. It feels that the position of "everybody gets the same rate on a job" can be carried to its illogical conclusion of "everybody gets the same rate regardless of job." It states that if the principle of job differentiation is sound, then individual differentiation within the job is also sound. Management argues that the single-wage rate on any particular job will reduce efficiency since the monetary stimulant for individual improvement on that job will be gone.

The union has pressed for the single-wage rate not because it is opposed to individuality, but rather because it mistrusts management methods for measurement and reward of individual differences. The story of merit rating, or man rating as it is sometimes called, is very similar to the history of abuse and misuse of other scientific management tools. Too often has merit rating resulted in wage increases to "stooges," "apple polishers," and "union busters." Too often has the technique of merit rating been used to "water down" wage rates by keeping all workers at a bottom wage level. Labor's opposition, therefore, flows from its experiences. Although in theory labor may accept the principle of individuality, in practice labor actively opposes it.

Sound wage policy requires acceptance of individuality in industry. Labor will have to preach and practice the principle of individuality. That includes not only the acceptance of job differences, but also individual differences. Management can obtain labor's cooperation in this program by inviting labor to participate in the merit-rating program. Here again the joint approach to the scientific-management tool results in worker confidence and workshop harmony.

The merit-rating program has as its objective accurate measurement of individual performance. A man-measurement yardstick must be created that will be mutually acceptable. Union and management discuss the yardstick. The factors of quantity and quality of output are set down. The factor of "employee attitude," so obnoxious to labor, is explored. Finally, policy is agreed upon. The merit yardstick, rules for merit review, and all procedures pertaining to merit increases are formulated. The merit-rating policy is instituted and administered by management. The union does not participate in the actual merit rating. It does not apply the yardstick and judge individual worth. It does not determine who shall receive the merit increases. It does police the program so that everyone may be assured that the adopted policy is being followed.

Individuality in industry must underlie sound wage policy. Because it moves in the direction of individual reward, the technique of merit rating is an important part of wage policy. There may be, however, more satisfactory methods that can be developed to meet the objective of payment based upon the individual's contribution. The incentive-wage plan is one of these. Merit rating, incentive, or whatever new technique may evolve, no wage structure will bring employee satisfaction and production if it is not fairly based on just principles of individuality.

Individuality in industry also requires a maintenance of opportunity for job promotion. Everyone wants to get ahead. There is no reason why the factory should be the graveyard for ambition. Wage policy requires not only remuneration for superior performance, but also individual recognition through job promotion. Wage policy must outline the opportunities for advancement. It must let each individual know in clear-cut fashion how he can "get places" through his own efforts.

Job evaluation and individual performance rating are only techniques used to establish guides for the ultimate objective of fair and equitable wage payment. These managerial techniques are not ends in themselves. They provide only the facts and guideposts for intelligent union-management determination of wage assignments. Collective bargaining on wages continues as it has in the past. Wage discussions, however, are based upon the facts uncovered by the use of scientific methods. Wage schedules are drawn up on the basis of job relationships and not on notions and emotions. There is method and reason in the arguments advanced by both sides.

The joint approach to wage schedules and wage rules does not interfere with management's right or ability to manage. Union participation in job evaluation, merit-rating, wage assignment, and promotion rules merely establishes a mutually satisfactory set of rules. The foreman remains the departmental executive. He operates within a framework of "ground rules" as he has always done. That those rules are now democratically arrived at does not alter his function in any way. The foreman and the worker retain their functional relationships.

The steward now bases his grievances upon factual data. He bases his arguments for promotions or wage increases upon clear-cut job definitions, systematic job relationships, and predetermined rules. The previous unsatisfactory methods of grappling with generalities are eliminated. A determination to fight is replaced by a determination of what is right.

Having achieved a framework of job alignment and wage rules, discussion on the problem of "adequate" wages can really take place. The adequate wage issue then becomes a question of increasing labor's standard of living and labor's share of the nation's gross product. Profit situations, general economic conditions, prices, productivity, and the general state of the nation decide the matter of the "adequate" wage. Thus, union and management, accepting the individuality principle and agreeing on the methods of measurement of individual differences, remove the wage structure from the area of union-management controversy in the factory and lay the foundation for efficiency advances.

High productivity and high worker morale are irrevocably dependent upon each other. The joint approach for productivity increase will succeed only in that factory, mill, or mine in which high morale exists. A jointly determined wage policy, based upon individuality in industry, yields the high PMH environment. It also yields the harmonious environment essential to successful collective bargaining.

CHAPTER IX

WHY DOESN'T THE GOVERNMENT DO SOMETHING?

Everybody says that the government should have a constructive labor policy. Everybody is right. The government's policy on industrial relations will greatly determine the future of our economy. Production plus democracy is the labor policy that will make the country strong. Government can do much to make this policy its own.

In the last decade government's industrial-relations policy has consisted principally in supporting the right of workers to organize into unions of their own choosing. The Wagner Act provides the secret employee election for determination of collective bargaining agent. Union-management negotiations are compulsory where workers vote union. Worker freedom in industry is thus established. *Human rights in the factory is now Federal policy. And government must continue to demand the unconditional acceptance of the Union by Industry.*

The adoption by government of the concept of ever-increasing production per man-hour is the next step in completing its industrial-relations policy for the plant level. It will implement the "production" half of production with freedom.

As pointed out earlier, the advocacy of productivity is an important element in the successful formulation of labor-management policy. Any arrangement for permanent stability in the factory must be in harmony with mass production, the cornerstone of modern industrial society. *It is, therefore, a responsibility of government to promote labor's acceptance of productivity, just as it is government's responsibility to promote industry's acceptance of the union.*

Government can encourage labor's acceptance of increased

output.   It can educate labor to understand that expanded productivity benefits all of society.   It can create worker confidence in scientific management by promoting research aimed at perfecting modern managerial techniques.   It can promote, through conference and contact, the concept of ever increasing PMH as our way of industrial life.   Such activity by government can assure labor's acceptance of productivity and production with freedom as America's industrial-relations policy.   Actually, government's promotion of production as a contribution to labor-management peace would be its secondary function.   Its primary function would be a contribution to all America by helping industry produce more for less.

Leadership and assistance by government in the field of productive efficiency is not new.   America's farmers can testify to that.   In these days of heated debate on the role of government in a free-enterprise economy, the farmer, our most rugged individualist, agrees that there is no disputing the positive contribution of the Department of Agriculture.   This government department with its assistance on the efficiency front has strengthened individual enterprise and initiative.   What government has done for the farm, it can do for industry.

The Department of Agriculture is one of America's best examples of how government can and should function in a democracy.   As a research and service institution it helps the farmer solve his daily, practical problems of production. By providing scientific bases for efficiency, it assists the farmer to obtain a higher yield per acre and more dairy and meal products for each pound of feed.   Science and practice are brought together in field and forest so that farmers may lower production costs and improve the quality of their products.   The activities of the Department of Agriculture have a genuine bread-and-butter meaning to the farmers of America.

While the Department of Agriculture is divided for administrative purpose into numerous specialized bureaus, research is the foundation of all its activity. One of these bureaus is devoted entirely to the study of farm machinery, processing equipment, work methods, farm electrification, and farm operating efficiency. The investigations in this field have resulted in the development of a number of mechanical devices that are now in mass production for farm use. This mass production has resulted in the lowering of cost of production of such major crops as corn, cotton, and sugar beets.

Another bureau has conducted special research in the field of plants and soils. There are some two hundred experimental and testing field stations scattered throughout the country. Increased productivity is sought through improved methods of crop growing, handling, and transportation. Explorers are sent to the remote parts of the world to seek superior plants for the American farmer. This exploration and experimentation has had practical results. A few years ago sugar-cane production faced extinction. Our entire crop was being ravaged by mosaic and other diseases. The department went to work on the problem. New disease-resistant varieties of cane were developed. Farmers received the new cane and planting went forward. The result is an annual harvest of nearly one-half million tons of cane.

The various problems of livestock improvement are continually being solved by the department's experimental farms and laboratories. Some 6,500 employees are in the field studying methods of livestock breeding and disease elimination. With the aim of improving the quality and palatability of meat, research is also conducted in the effects of chilling, ripening, curing, smoking, and storing of meat.

Farm-work simplification is one of the department's newest projects. This research in best work methods is being directed by Purdue University. The research study is known as the National Farm Work Simplification Project. The government has assigned $87,400 to finance the project. Purdue, in cooperation with twelve other colleges, is applying scientific study and analysis to farm work. The project is developing improved methods of doing the many jobs associated with agricultural production. Production per man-hour is constantly increasing as a result of this practical research and experimentation.

As a part of the national research on work simplification a study was made of methods used in producing celery plants. The job required about seventy hours of man-labor per acre of set celery. Work simplification reduced time requirements as much as 50 per cent. This information has been vividly portrayed in a motion picture entitled "Celery Seedbags." The movie is being shown to the nation's farmers.

Research in farm equipment, crops, livestock, and work methods is only a part of a national program, which includes 8,500 projects. These projects are receiving the scientific approach at research stations, experimental farms, and universities located in all parts of the country. This search for knowledge has the single objective of benefiting all America by bringing the facts to the farmer.

Bringing the facts to the farmer—teaching the farmer the best way to farm—is the function of the Extension Division of the department. This division has been in operation for over thirty years and employs 10,000 men and women. It is a transmission belt from research and experimental centers to the farmer, and from farmer to the fact-finding centers. Through publications, radio, motion pictures, exhibits, community conferences, classrooms, and personal contact, a tremendous quantity of accurate and useful knowledge is brought to the farm.

The government's transmission belt of production knowledge operates through the 3,000 county agents. The county agent as the salesman of efficiency is known intimately to every farmer in the nation. His routine takes him to each farm in his county. He translates scientific research and experimental findings in such a way that farm people can adopt or reject them. He is the man-on-the-spot who helps the farmer meet his problem. Is the farmer confused on costs because his simple bookkeeping system doesn't meet the needs of his rapidly expanding farm? The county agent has just the booklet and sample forms on farm cost accounting. Is the farmer worried about getting the most out of his new combine? The county agent may suggest his attending a combine class, which would be organized for some Saturday afternoon. Has the farmer some fruit trees? The county agent sends him a series of reminders giving the dates for spraying the trees to control insect destruction. Ever-increasing farm efficiency is the government's business, and the county agent is there to persuade, to demonstrate, to cooperate, and to guide the farmer toward better farming.

There is no single government agency performing for industry the job that the Department of Agriculture is doing for the farmer. There is no office in the industrial community that serves the manager in the same way that the county agent serves the farmer. America needs the early establishment of an Agency to Promote Efficiency in Industry.

Such an agency might become a part of the Department of Commerce. The new Department of Commerce and Industry might duplicate for the industrial world what is being done by the Department of Agriculture. However, since productivity demands worker participation and cooperation, perhaps an Interdepartmental Committee, consisting of representatives of the Commerce and Labor Departments, should establish this agency for efficiency promotion. Perhaps a new and independent agency, responsible to Congress itself, might be created. Whatever the organizational and administrative structure, government leadership and assistance are necessary if we are to realize our productive potential.

Government promulgation of productivity would not necessitate new and revolutionary government action. It would not require a tremendous increase of personnel or expense. Actually there are already in existence the agencies that could provide the basis for a federal campaign for PMH. Some are prewar agencies. Some were created as a result of war necessities and now are disestablished. If these various agencies were gathered together they could form the beginnings of our government program for efficiency promotion in industry.

An example of what government could do in the field of industrial efficiency was furnished by an agency called Training Within Industry. The Training Within Industry program was one of our most effective wartime agencies. Now that the war is ended, Training Within Industry is no longer part of our federal services. This agency performed a remarkable service to the cause of industrial efficiency. Proceeding on the premise that better foremanship is an important key to greater production, it trained over one and one half million foremen and supervisors in some 16,000 plants. Directors of the program were Channing Dooley of the Socony-Vacuum Company and Walter Dietz of Western Electric. These men were borrowed from their companies in 1940 to head up the agency that helped industry help itself. Dooley and Dietz, with a staff of 392 men and women in 110 industrial cities have made a lasting contribution to industrial progress. Their slogan of "Efficiency through Better Foremanship" became a reality.

Training Within Industry, (or TWI), was a program of teaching supervisors the techniques of getting the workers to do better jobs. Efficient foremanship requires a knowledge of the immediate work. The welding foreman must know welding; the die-making foreman, die making. The foreman must also have a knowledge of his company's policies, departmental relationships, union agreement, and other "ground rules." These two "knowledges" are peculiar to each company and must be taught by the company. There are three other requisites for successful foremanship. These three skills are general in nature and apply to supervision everywhere. These skills must be acquired. They are the three "R's" of foremanship. This is where TWI entered the picture.

TWI taught the foreman to apply the techniques of the three skills—*job instruction, job methods,* and *job relations.* Foremen must know how to instruct. The working force reflects the instruction it has received. Workers instructed properly give more production and less scrap. Other results are fewer accidents and less tool-and-equipment damage. The skill of *job instruction* is necessary for successful foremanship.

Foremen must become methods-conscious. Thousands of jobs are being done the way they are done simply because they got started that way. Many people never question the current method—just keep on in the old way. The development of improvements does not require inventive genius, but it does require the questioning attitude. The foreman learns to look critically at all jobs he directs not just once, but repeatedly and constantly. TWI Job Methods program was a condensed, hard-hitting use of the managerial tool, work simplification. The skill of methods improvement had to be learned by the foreman if he was to contribute fully to productivity.

Full productive effort comes only when the supervisor becomes the leader of the workers he directs. This is a recognition of the human factor in production. Working with people is a skill that can be acquired. It reduces misunderstandings, grievances, and brings teamwork into the department. TWI taught the elements of sound *job relations on the job.*

The results of foreman training in the skills of job instruction, job methods, and job relations were outstanding. Each of the techniques contributed in its own special way to increased production per man-hour. A brass manufacturing company reported its experience on one operation, that of turning out 9,600 pieces every eight hours. Before foreman training in job instruction, scrap averaged 1,770 pieces per eight hours. After the training, scrap was reduced to 25 pieces. After further application of job instruction scrap was reduced to 5 pieces in 20,000. A cement company stated that job methods training developed an improved method of feeding cement sacks into a cleaner and saved 35 miles of walking per day for some 70 girl employees. A steel plant wrote that the job relations program resulted in a 54 per cent drop in grievances and complaints. Prior to foreman training, the plant grievance committee met at least three times a week. Afterward it met on the average of three times a month.

These experiences were not isolated. They were verified by a survey of 1,000 companies that used TWI. That list read like a *Who's Who in American Industry*. Out of the thousand companies that reported, 760 reported a greater than 25 per cent production increase, and 650 reported that grievances were reduced by more than 25 per cent. The three skills of efficient supervision were an "Open Sesame" to a vast production potential.

The fame of TWI spread abroad. The British Government, hearing of the program, sent a representative to this country to investigate. He spent six months studying the details. Upon his return to England the program was instituted there. By the war's end over 10,000 foremen in the British Isles had received instruction in the three supervisory skills.

TWI was one government agency that was accepted wholeheartedly by industry. During 1944 the National Association of State Chambers of Commerce awarded its "Industry Award" to TWI. This was the first instance of the decoration of a government agency by private industry. Industry opinion was reflected by the statement of H. E. Blythe, vice-president and general manager of Goodyear Aircraft Corporation.

We have no hesitation in stating that the TWI program has been a most valuable aid. One of its most valuable features is the naturalness of the application to shop problems. We look upon the TWI program not just as a wartime expedient, but intend to make it an important part of our permanent activity.

The three skills of *instruction, methods,* and *relations* must be extended to every American plant. The three "R's" must reach not only the foreman, but also every worker. Further, the program, by embodying union participation, can get even better results. This program and its staff should become an integral part of government's promotion of efficiency in industry.

The War Production Board's division of Labor-Management Production Committees was another agency that deserved continuation. This agency published a newspaper, *Labor-Management News,* devoted entirely to production promotion. Pamphlets, posters, movies, and radio were all used for the same objective.

Representatives of the agency visited factories to discuss the experiences of the some 5,000 plant committees. They developed the technique of the joint approach to productivity increase. In spite of many handicaps this agency performed well. Its work should be continued. The promotion of production committees might become another important part of government action on production.

Another agency that would fit into our suggested program is the Technical Division of the Department of Labor's Conciliation Service. This division is making available to union and management information on management techniques. It stands ready to assist on any problem arising from labor-management differences on job evaluation, time study, or other managerial controls. Unfortunately the Technical Division has only made a start. A great deal of work needs to be done. Impartial information on the latest developments in job evaluation, time study, and other scientific management techniques must become available to unions and employers alike.

Training Within Industry, Labor-management Production Committees, and the Technical Division of the Department of Labor's Conciliation Service are only a few of the activities that could be properly carried on by a permanent agency for efficiency in industry.   Government, in addition to these activities, could promote a real program of research. There is a need for basic research in the science of management.   National projects to perfect and simplify the techniques of time study, motion economy, and job evaluation are an immediate necessity.   The methods of scientific management must become a part of the operation of every enterprise.   In addition, constant development of productive techniques and technology is a national "must."   Government should assume its responsibility for the stimulation of such research.   What government support for research has done for farm technology, it can do for industrial technology.

An agency for industrial efficiency would not be a remote institution serving some vague purpose.   It would help management and labor to solve the practical, day-to-day problems of factory production.   It would stimulate the production of more goods for less cost.   It would supplement full employment programs by recommending legislation that would encourage everincreasing output per labor-hour.   The stimulation of productivity is the kind of government "assistance" all America will welcome.

It is interesting to note that other major powers are giving their attention to productivity.   Russia's Stakhanovite movement is but one example.   Recently Britian's Labor government has moved on this front.   On March 3, 1946 Prime Minister Atlee in a national broadcast called upon trade unionists to drop any "customs or rules" that might hamper full production and employers to "throw aside any restrictions of output calculated to create artificial shortages."   Three days later a great conference of 1,600 union officials was held in London to discuss frankly with the Prime Minister and other Cabinet officials the practical steps that unions could take to make the government's production drive a success. On the following day, a similar conference was held between representatives of all the main employers' associations and the government. Both conferences were followed by meetings of a similar type in the principal industrial centers throughout Britain. Britain is becoming productivity-conscious.

In contrast, look at our government's policy on productivity. Did you know that the use of the latest in managerial techniques is prohibited in Army and Navy industrial operations? Did you know that time study is banned by Congressional act from the shipbuilding yards operated by the Navy? How can government encourage labor's acceptance of time study in industry when it prohibits it in its own factories? How can the automobile industry sell incentives to the CIO-UAW when government prohibits incentives in Army arsenals? This situation, understandable when it originated some thirty years ago, is allowed to continue year after year because Congress itself does not understand modern managerial tools.

This year Congress, once again, renewed Section 2 of the Military Appropriations Act prohibiting time study and incentive-wage payment plans in military enterprises. A study of the Congressional Record indicates the job of education if government is to promote productivity. All the old arguments of "speed-up" and "stretch-out" are in the record. Can one blame labor for its attitudes if one hears the same arguments on the floor of the Senate? Typical was Senator Magnuson's remark: "All intelligent students of labor, management, and capital have long since abandoned such systems (time study and incentives) in this country in their dealings with their working people."

The Senators who voted to continue the prohibition of time study based their action on a report of the Senate's Education and Labor Committee submitted in 1912. That report, in its entirety, is incorporated in the 1945–1946 Congressional Record. It is astounding in its charges against scientific management.   And it is astounding that this report is accepted as a modern commentary on time study and incentives.   Before government can sell productivity techniques to the nation's employers and workers it must first put its own house in order.   The elimination of legislative restrictions on time study is long overdue.

By accepting the responsibility of promoting labor's acceptance of productivity techniques, government will round out its factory level industrial-relations policy. Government, by assisting management and union to travel together the production road, will help bring harmony to industry.   Ever-increasing PMH is a community of interest that can yield high profits, high wages, and industrial peace.

Government must help put *production* into *production with freedom.*

CHAPTER X

DON'T WORK YOURSELF
OUT OF A JOB!

Look at the windshield wiper on your car. It is a typical example of this age of specialization and mass production. Millions of wipers are turned out in rapid-fire order. Each worker doing a single repetitive operation permits the complex windshield wiper to become a practical production item. The mass-production wiper, handle, carburetor, engine, tire make the low-cost car possible. It would be impossible for one man alone to get the materials, machine the parts, and assemble the automatic wiper. Mass production, with its division of labor, has freed man from his grinding struggle with nature for survival. But it has also made it difficult for the great mass of workers to grasp the direct relation of their own productivity to their standards of living.

In a simple economy man can view directly the results of his own efforts. He increases his productivity and the result in increased living standard is immediate. The early American homesteaders wove their own cloth, churned their own butter, cured their own meat, "raised" their own bread. They knew that the more they produced, the more they had, and the better they lived. In our complex social organization the immediate job and the net result may be very remote. It is difficult for the worker making the rubber blade for windshield wipers to understand why more blades per hour mean a better life for all. On the contrary, he *believes*, on the basis of his past experience, that more blades per hour mean less hours of pay. Thus it is easy to realize why the modern worker accepts the reasoning of "Don't work too fast—you may work yourself out of a job."

In prewar industry the auto-parts worker reasoned that

there were only so many million automobiles to be built that year. He concluded that the more he turned out in a day, the less days he would work. This belief that there are only so many jobs and only so much production is the "road to scarcity" practices. The war years temporarily dissipated this kind of thinking. When there are jobs for all, scarcity arguments lose their force. But let the first shadows of unemployment fall, and labor will return to its past thinking and practice. No amount of argument or logic will prevail. Joe Workman may nod his head in agreement to the productivity arguments, but his actions will be dictated by what, to him, will be the logic of "Don't work yourself out of a job."

He will agree that production with freedom may be the answer to a sound labor-management relationship. He will accept PHM as the key to a good life for all. He will tell you that he is for productivity for it is synonomous with progress. But after all this, *unless there is an abundance of jobs* he will return to scarcity practices. He will be a passive resistance movement of one. And the "ones" will be in the millions. His driving force will be fear—the fear of unemployment. We shall be caught in a vicious circle of *no jobs without productivity and no productivity without jobs*. And there can be no industrial peace in this kind of situation.

Jobs for all is the necessary environment if production with freedom is to flourish. Just talking about industrial efficiency will not achieve it. Management and labor must have a common will and purpose to work together for it. That common purpose can survive only in a full-employment economy. It will be an almost impossible task to sell productivity with millions of men idle. The man at the machine slows down to "protect" his job when he sees long lines at the employment office.

Thus we arrive at the simple proposition, that if production with freedom is to become a reality in the factory, business will have to turn to the problem of achieving full employment with the same zeal and ingenuity with which it tackles the problems of production and sales.

Much has been said and written on this matter of full employment. The roles of government, business, labor, and agriculture in a jobs-for-all economy have been examined. Legislation on the subject has been enacted and more is pending. There is a great deal of energy being expended in the exploration of this new economic horizon. The problem of full employment is not the subject of this book, but having said that full employment is an essential for a functioning production with freedom, there is an obligation to emphasize the role of the individual manager if full employment is to be achieved. Putting it bluntly, the business leader must begin to widen the dimensions of his own economic thinking. It is time to recognize that decisions made at the factory level reverberate throughout the economy. It is the manager's duty, therefore, to do what he can to aid an expanding economy. There is an urgent need for business statesmanship in the factories of America.

The individual manager who desires to practice this statesmanship must first face the reality that mass production cannot continue without mass consumption. Full employment is, in a large measure, dependent upon an ever-increasing consumption by more and more people. But that goal is not easy to achieve. It puts the goal of increasing purchasing power alongside the goal of increasing profits. It will take unusual business acumen to blend the drive for profits with the broad responsibility for an ever-rising living standard for the masses of people. But it must be accomplished.

The acceptance of the principle of mass consumption, when translated into action at the plant level, means the introduction of new thinking and new techniques. That it can be done is evidenced by the new trends in some sections of industry. More and more managers are advocating a mass-pricing policy. More and more managers are advocating a high-wage policy. Both are necessary to mass consumption.

The individual manager can assist in the achievement of a full-employment economy. He can take the long range point of view on business practices. There is a battle between two philosophies of doing business—profits through production or profits through restriction. The modern business leader must choose. The Restrictionist takes the existing American market and tries to wring the most out of it. The Expansionist makes his ever-decreasing prices a bid for an ever-increasing American market. He bids for profits through volume sales and low prices. Thus he contributes to mass consumption.

The individual manager, in addition, can underwrite mass consumption by endorsing such aids as minimum wage levels, annual wages, and profit sharing. Business must understand that the worker is also its best customer. Business leaders have another task. They will have to remove business-created barriers to production expansion. This will be the acid test of business statesmanship. The frontier for more goods for less can be exploited only if the "economic toll bridges" are removed. Business if it desires to lead to an expanding economy, must abolish such devices as patent "control" where they are used to "peg production." Business must cleanse itself of retarding abuses. It cannot sincerely ask labor to practice productivity unless it also moves in this direction. If business expects labor to choose the production highway and eschew restriction, it must do the same.

There is still another test for the modern business statesman. Full employment cannot be achieved unless there is conscious cooperation between business and government. Business must recognize that it cannot achieve full employment without government coordination and direction. In our mass-production age business by itself cannot solve all the problems necessary to maintain continuous high level production. No single entrepreneur can guarantee steady jobs to his employees. That is admitted by business, whose arguments against the annual wage openly states that the individual firm cannot assume the liability in such a giant risk. No single firm, or for that matter, no group of firms, can guarantee indefinitely a level of output that will keep all America employed. Industry, no matter how willing, cannot by itself meet the all-important issue of the boom-or-bust cycle. If business insists that it can, it will jeopardize the continuance of private endeavor as our economic way of life. The political and social implications of large-scale unemployment necessitates government action on the economic front. Beardsley Ruml, who is certainly not an advocate of the totalitarian economy, puts it this way:

> The problem of domestic recovery and long-term prosperity should no longer be so neglected nor should it be relegated to the private agencies of agriculture, labor, and business. Much as these private agencies can and must do, they cannot do all, indeed *they cannot even do their part*, without proper governmental leadership and cooperation.

The individual business leader, therefore, has a twofold task on this issue of government in business. First, he must rid himself of an unreasoning hostility to any and all government regulation. Second, he must accept the premise of government economic leadership as essential if full employment and prosperity for all are to be achieved and maintained.

The goal is an abundance of jobs at all times. To achieve this we need plant managers who will, individually and collectively, explore the frontier of mass consumption, remove business-created barriers to an expanding economy, accept the necessity for government economic leadership.

An excellent example of this kind of activity was shown

by Paul Hoffman's Committee for Economic Development. It was organized by businessmen, for businessmen, in the summer of 1942. Fifty thousand businessmen, large and small, in 2,000 cities and towns discussed a new kind of business leadership. The committee hired nationally famous economists and research experts to provide the guidance and information to a new understanding of private enterprise. Based upon that wide study, William Benton, vice-chairman of the committee, outlined a new set of guideposts for business leadership:

The free enterprise system is not, never has been, and never shall be a system of complete laissez faire. For instance it is:

not the freedom to seek profits by any and all means;

not the right to profit at the expense and the welfare of the community;

not the freedom of any man to exploit any other;

not the freedom to waste the natural resources of the country;

not the right to monopolize (which impedes or prevents the establishment of new businesses, creates scarcity, and imperils the spirit of enterprise);

not the opposition to necessary and appropriate government regulation or operation;

not the appeal to government for subsidy or protection when adversity appears.

Here is a broad outline for intelligent self-discipline for business, formulated by business. It can serve as the program for the business statesman.

It is imperative that industry organize itself around a philosophy of abundance. The vitality, sincerity, and intelligence that was exemplified by the Committee for Economic Development could well permeate the National Association of Manufacturers and the U. S. Chamber of Commerce. There is a need for a new and flexible business leadership, willing to tackle present problems in a fresh and bold way. It should educate the individual businessman to new business practices and motives. There is no blueprint of action. There is a guide to action. It is a sincere, high purpose to serve America and her people above all else. It is a firm resolve that the profit drive shall be in keeping with that high purpose. That is the least America expects from its businessmen. And it is the least the business leader must give if he wants productivity in his factory.

While a full-employment environment is essential to production with freedom, it should not be concluded that full employment is the one answer to all of our industrial relations problems.

Labor-management difficulties will not dissolve just because there is high-level production and an abundance of jobs. Also, all of these difficulties will not dissolve if we achieve production with freedom at the factory level. There is a range of national problems that goes beyond our immediate discussion. Take the matter of wage setting. The day of the free market establishing wage levels is over. The entrance of the national union brings up for reevaluation the problem of general wage levels. The effect on the economy of powerful unions establishing national wage scales needs to be explored. The relationship of productivity to wage levels needs amplifying. There is the problem of balancing wages, profits, and prices in order to get an expanding economy. The wage level does influence the profit and price level and brings up the old question of necessary business incentives. The general wage level and continuous employment are also interdependent, because of the effect of wages on prices and markets. In fact, there is no sector of our economy that is not affected by this problem.

There are some additional phases of this wage question. What about the problem of wage differentials between urban and rural areas; between North and South? If the cost of living is lower in the rural areas than in the city, should wages be correspondingly lower even though the same work is performed? And what about mobility of labor? What wage level will achieve the maximum of labor mobility necessary to an expanding economy? The answers to these questions need study and research for upon them depends the achievement of a sound economy.

One thing is clear. In the society that contains the powerful national union, the general wage problem is only one phase of the industrial relations problem. And there is no easy solution of the total industrial-relations problem in a democratic economy.

In the democratic economy the right to strike is proclaimed by all sides as a basic freedom. Yet, reconcile that freedom with the self-evident right of government to protect the economic structure when it is endangered by the exercise of the right to strike. It has been argued that the reconciliation lies in abridging the right of strike in vital services. What is not vitally necessary to the life of our economy in this technologically advanced era? Certainly the list of vital things includes transportation and communication. Then we must include coal and oil since they are vital to transportation. And should we not include meats and other food products as vital? In fact, a listing of vitally necessary things in this highly mechanized modern age would include the majority of industries and services. Does this mean, then, compulsory arbitration and the banning of all strikes? If so, what happens to our democratic economy?

It has been suggested that strike prevention rather than cure is the hope of our democracy; that the emphasis should be on avoiding the crisis of the national strike. This school emphasizes the establishment of national machinery for mediation, fact finding, and voluntary arbitration to prevent strikes from occurring, or being prolonged until they result in economic collapse. It is argued that this is the only answer possible if we desire to retain a democratic economy. And it is also argued that some strikes are the price of freedom.

Some employer groups argue that voluntary machinery for dispute settlement cannot work until the monopoly power of some national unions is broken. They maintain that present labor power is similar to the earlier monopoly power of unregulated capital, which placed group interest above national interest. They ask that this power be regulated and curtailed. The remedies they suggest vary from placing unions under the antitrust laws and prohibiting national bargaining to enforcing union "responsibility" through court action and penalties. Labor replies that it needs its power to balance corporate power and asks how it can be regulated without destroying its bargaining position and the conditions of genuinely fair collective bargaining.

There is an urgent need for a basic study of union, management, and government policies and practices on the subject of resolving employer-employee differences. Based upon such research, patterns of permissible action can be established to govern the group relations that dominate our economic life. Union and corporation activities need channeling if we are to resolve economic differences without tearing apart the economy. This field of group relations, which might be termed the "politics of economics," should command the attention of our experts. For the total problem of industrial relations will not be solved until we understand the "politics of economics."

The total industrial relations problem is outside the scope of this book. The "politics of economics" on the plant level is our subject. Thus, for our purposes it is sufficient to point out that while full employment will not resolve, by itself, all labor-management conflict, it is necessary to the achievement of production with freedom in the factory.

Full employment is the assurance both to capital and labor that it will not work itself out of business opportunities nor jobs.   An abundance of jobs will facilitate productivity acceptance.   Business, by helping to maintain a full employment economy will create the atmosphere in which ever-increasing productivity can be practiced. Production with freedom will flourish.   Stability in the factory will be assured.   Production per man-hour will increase, and with it the nation's standard of living will rise.

CHAPTER XI

STRAWS IN THE WIND

Our national labor relations—be they peaceful and stable or belligerent and chaotic—are the sum total of thousands and thousands of plant-level relationships. And the answer to the plant relationship is the development of self-government through constructive collective bargaining. There is nothing new in this answer. And certainly it does not need emphasis. What does need emphasis, however, is first, that collective bargaining can succeed only if labor and management are in common agreement upon the basic tenets of living together, and second, that these basic tenets are embodied in production with freedom. Without such a common approach, industrial self-government is doomed to failure.

Let labor and management pursue their own objectives; let each press its own interest, but unless they do so within a framework of common agreement on production with freedom, they cannot resolve harmoniously their daily differences. This is the experience of hundreds of plants which have successful labor-management relations. It is also the experience of the Toledo Labor-Management-Citizens Committee.

The Toledo Labor-Management-Citizens Committee, or the L-M-C, as it is known locally, was officially formed on Nov. 20, 1945. Since that time it has received nation-wide publicity. Articles describing the Committee have appeared in newspapers from coast to coast. The skeptical Associated Press sent its national labor reporter, Max Hall, to Toledo to investigate. He described the Toledo plan in glowing terms in a series of three articles. The Hearst chain did the same and described the Toledo story in eight articles. Other prominent newspapers sent their labor

111

editors. All agreed that the Toledo plan worked. Such
widely separated newspapers, both in geography and in
viewpoint, as the Detroit *News*, the Washington *Post*,
the St. Louis *Post-Dispatch*, and the Louisville *Courier-
Journal* suggested editorially that their committees could
well emulate Toledo. Louisville did, and an L-M-C is
functioning there.

"Grass-roots innovation," "pacesetter in industrial
harmony," "blueprint for industrial peace," were some of
the heads on national magazine articles, including the
widely circulated *Reader's Digest* and the intellectual New
York *Times* Sunday Magazine. The Toledo plan was even
the subject of a Gallup poll. This famous opinion-gather-
ing agency related that in Toledo many labor disputes had
been settled or averted by the efforts of the L-M-C, and
asked this question of the nation, including a cross section
of union members:

In Toledo, Ohio, strikes have been settled by a local
committee of citizens. Do you think that this method
would work in your community?

This poll was taken in November, 1946, one year after
the Toledo L-M-C was formed. The results of this nation-
wide survey showed only 23 per cent voting against the
plan. Apparently America felt the Toledo plan was
one solution to labor-management difficulties.

While newspaper and magazine articles and editorials
all agreed on the merits of the plan, they differed on the
reasons for its success. Some said that the plan worked
because the community's top management and top labor
leaders participated. Others, that the local harmony
between AFL and CIO did the trick. Still others talked
about the community's participation through its six public
representatives as the key. One article emphasized the
fact that the L-M-C was, in effect, a city department
and was subsidized by tax funds. An employer magazine

argued that enlightened employers in Toledo were responsible. And from the people it questioned, the Gallup poll drew this reason for the plan's success: "Local people understand local conditions better than outsiders."

All the commentators were correct. Each of the reasons given has contributed its share to the success of the Toledo plan. But the basic reason for the effectiveness of the L-M-C has been lost in the brightness of the national spotlight which seeks news in personalities rather than principles.

What is the Toledo plan? The idea is simple enough. It is a community mediation board of eighteen members representing equally labor, management, and public. It not only acts in strike situations but also attempts to avert shutdowns. It does this in two ways. First, by remaining in constant touch, through its members, with the industrial relations situations in all of Toledo's workshops, and second, by a well-planned strike prevention program of education beamed at the whole community but particularly at foremen and stewards. Here the community's mass communication media as well as forums, conferences, and institutes are used. Sound labor relations is the community's business and the L-M-C operates on that principle. Up to here, one could well say that there is nothing startling or new in the Toledo plan. But there is more to the L-M-C than meets the eye.

To find the basic reason for the success of the Toledo plan we must go back to April, 1945, some seven months before the L-M-C was officially formed. It was then that six CIO and AFL leaders first met with an equal number of important employer and public representatives to discuss generally the topic of labor-management relations. There was no thought of a permanent board or committee. There was no thought of a specific plan for strike prevention or strike settlement. In fact, all sides agreed that current disputes were not to be discussed. What strikes occurred as the months of meetings went by were of no concern to the group.   The group confined itself to a discussion of the general problems of labor-management relations.   As the discussions continued, guiding principles of sound industrial relations evolved.   What was happening was that this group was coming slowly to an agreement on a general code of conduct for labor, for management.   They had reversed the usual union-management procedure of agreeing on self-government and then trying to decide on the principles by which they would govern themselves.   For these men, through their exchange of opinions and experiences, had come to the conclusion that while industrial harmony depended upon industrial self-government there could be no such self-government without a common agreement on the principles of living together.

Many times during the days of discussion in those seven months, it looked as if no agreement could be reached; as if there were fundamental differences.   But by November, labor and management in Toledo had unanimously endorsed a set of principles which would guide their relationship in the plants of their community.   Those principles were embodied in a charter and upon that foundation the L-M-C was created.

It is this charter that accounts for the success of the Toledo plan.   And its importance is not underrated by those who wrote it, for it is an essential part of the Toledo plan that no union or management shall have access to the L-M-C services unless they first endorse the charter.   Led by the affirmative action of the local Chamber of Commerce and the central bodies of CIO and AFL, plant after plant, and local union after local union, are discussing the charter and adopting it as their code of conduct. And should the individual plant management or local union stray from the tenets of the charter, the L-M-C has the power to take the charter from the offending member. It is this common agreement on principles that makes the L-M-C click, that unites Toledo labor and management leadership. And the Toledo charter spells out the philosophy of production with freedom.

Take the preamble of the Toledo charter. It clearly states that the purpose of the committee is

> To jointly seek successful patterns of democratic economic living and to achieve self-government in industry. . . .

Here at the outset, both sides accept democracy in industry as their starting point. They announce that the industrial relations answer is self-government. The collective bargaining technique is endorsed. Toledo's employers declare, in effect, that unions are a part of the industrial scene and that management must accept all the implications of that fact.

Production comes in for its share of attention and the charter makes it clear that the philosophy of productive efficiency and technological advance must be accepted by labor.

Production with freedom is the foundation of the Toledo plan. And no similar plan will work without these principles as a guide to action. Let those communities which desire to follow Toledo get agreement on principles from "all hands" before they put out on the rough sea of dispute settlement.

Simultaneously with the Toledo meetings, another venture in getting agreement upon principles was being tried nationally. Forward-looking Eric Johnston, then president of the United States Chamber of Commerce, had invited William Green, president of the AFL, and Phillip Murray, president of the CIO, to meet with him and a few other industrialists to determine if postwar labor-management clashes could be averted.

The Johnston-Murray-Green meetings were not collective bargaining conferences but were actually the first attempt to get agreement on a national code of conduct. What was occurring in Toledo, Eric Johnston was attempting nationally. Neither group knew what the other was doing. Both had come to the conclusion independently that without a basic charter of principles to guide daily industrial living, no lasting peace could be achieved.

On Mar. 28, 1945, these three national leaders of business and labor announced agreement upon a code of principles and a plan to establish a national committee of labor and business to achieve industrial harmony upon the foundation of their agreed-upon code. It is interesting to note that the Johnston-Murray-Green code also embodied the production with freedom principles. It called for the acceptance of worker freedom by management and stated that "improved productive efficiency and technological advancement must be constantly encouraged."

The Johnston-Murray-Green charter made industrial relations history. The charter was endorsed by the United States Chamber of Commerce, the national AFL, and the CIO. The joint committee which was to put the plan into operation, however, did not materialize. The AFL Executive Council, while endorsing the charter, instructed its president not to participate in any follow-up meetings in which the CIO was present. This AFL action ended the possibility of effectuating the charter. In addition, the National Association of Manufacturers had not helped by its refusal to participate. Nevertheless, the charter marked a milestone, and eventually labor and management must return to its principles or face the alternative of industrial "peace" enforced by a police state. As the Providence *Journal* editorialized about the charter,

> In its broad sweep and sound philosophy it is an essay in human freedom and as such it deserves to be hailed and praised. It is a powerful answer to those here and abroad who say fatalistically that more State control and collectivism is inevitable.

The charter failed because certain sections of business and labor had not yet accepted the philosophy of democracy and production. Where that philosophy has been accepted by both sides, collective bargaining is yielding results.

The classic examples of constructive collective bargaining are in the women's and men's clothing industry. Here the unions, one an AFL affiliate and one belonging to CIO, are the outstanding labor exponents of ever-increasing productivity. And on the other hand, management has accepted unions as an integral part of these industries for over twenty-five years.

That production with freedom is the difference between industrial warfare and industrial peace is evidenced from recent experiences in the steel and automobile industries. Steel and auto, up to 1935, were open-shop industries. Open and hidden labor-management warfare, including violent strikes and lockouts, the use of spies and stooges, of guns and gas, were commonplace in these two industries. At the present time, steel is not only well organized but also offers a good example of management and labor accepting the principles of constructive collective bargaining. True, there are still threats from both sides. True, there are possibilities of open warfare here and there in the different branches of the steel industry. But, on the whole, the approach of the United States Steel Corporation and the approach of the United Steelworkers to their relationship is in the direction of enlarging the field of understanding and cooperation.

A somewhat different situation exists in the automobile industry. There, too, the violent period of the sitdown strikes in 1934 and 1935 was followed by a rapid unionization program. There, too, collective agreements have been concluded. Somehow, however, these attempts at self-government have not brought industrial peace. Somehow both labor and management are known to have found ways of avoiding the peaceful method, with labor constantly resorting to wildcat strikes or management driving labor to the point where the strike becomes the only way out.

Why has collective bargaining taken one turn in the

case of steel and a somewhat different turn in the case of automobiles? Many reasons could be given. But, fundamentally, the answer is that both steel management and steel labor are in agreement upon principles of democratic industrial living and they are developing patterns of self-government. They are moving in the direction of production with freedom. They have accepted the proposition that productive efficiency and freedom in the factory are not only compatible, but the solid bed rock upon which lasting industrial self-government must be built. This is, as yet, not the situation in the automobile industry.

The Toledo plan, the Johnston-Murray-Green charter, and the collective contracts in the clothing industries are straws in the wind. More and more charters will be written. And more and more, the philosophy of production with freedom will permeate our industrial community.

CHAPTER XII

CONCLUSION

There is no doubt that the founding fathers would marvel at today's America. But we have paid a price for our material progress. It is now completely true that no man is an island unto himself. The relative dependence of the individual on others—and on the society itself—to supply even his simplest necessities is now a *fact of life*. Our economy has given us material abundance and increased leisure, but it has taken from us, with our blessing and consent, the power to provide for ourselves. Self-sufficiency for the individual, the community, or the group in our modern society is as bygone as the traveling tinker.

A relatively few men absent from their workplaces can stop the flow of our economy. Materials and parts absent from their work places can do the same. This was demonstrated during World War II when the rubber shortage was at its peak. The nation's dairy products supply was seriously threatened by a shortage of small rubber rings for cream separators. Lack of tiny copper screws, immediately after the war, kept thousands of floor lamps unfinished and gathering dust in factory storerooms. Hundreds of examples could be listed. And they all add up to one thing. America's factories, mills, mines, and farms are one giant assembly line.

There is nothing so dramatic as an electricity shutdown to bring our economic interdependence sharply to our attention. A power strike—or a breakdown in a power system if it should continue over any sustained period—can result in tremendous losses and inconveniences to people who have no connection with the shutdown.

Transportation tieups go along with power tieups in their serious economic consequences. A sleet storm, a tornado, a blizzard, a lockout, or a strike can make hundreds of thousands of people helpless and destitute. This could never have happened to our great-grandparents. Oil trucks, for instance, can't get through and homes grow desperately cold. Great-grandfather had his shed handy at the backdoor, and the fireplace worked even if it did smoke.

None of us, however, would trade places with great-grandfather. He was self-reliant and self-sustaining. But his supply of food, clothing, and shelter was meager and insecure. We have traded great-grandfather's self-reliance and self-sustenance for interdependence with its abundance. Life's necessities can flow to us in constant supply only as the complex and interwoven society we have built runs smoothly without loose monkey wrenches jamming the gears.

Along with the development of our technology have come new social institutions. The rise of the corporation was the outstanding fact of the eighties and nineties. The rise of the union was just as inevitable, with associations of workers following the rise of group enterprise as night follows day. The growth of the trade union from the status of an outlaw organization into an indispensable part of the working machinery of our society is now another fact of life.

Unions have grown like magic plants under the wand of a magician. In the last fifteen years, union membership in America has increased from 3 million to 15 million and there is every evidence that this growth will continue. There is no more sound talk about "getting rid" of unions. Unions are here to stay, just as management is here to stay, and we must face the social implications of this fact.

Unions and collective bargaining are a normal manifestation of a democratic industrial society. Under modern conditions of corporate enterprise it must be recognized that the individual is in a poor position to bargain for the best possible return for his services. Association for bargaining purposes is the inevitable development.

But men do not join unions only for wage bargaining. They want industrial democracy. They want a say in their economic destiny. And the individual who has achieved political citizenship will not be content with anything less than full economic citizenship. The democratic answer to this worker urge is collective bargaining. It is the democratic technique by which it is hoped harmonious and fruitful labor-management relations can be realized in the mass production society.

Democracy in industry—free collective bargaining—is inevitable in a political democracy. Any attempt to frustrate worker efforts for industrial democracy can lead only to the destruction of capitalism. Workers, using their political democracy, will call upon government to regulate industry. They will demand that government fix wages and other conditions of employment. The participation in industry which the worker could not achieve through the collective bargaining process he will attempt to achieve indirectly through government action. It is of little avail to tell workers that the total regulation of business must lead inevitably to the total regulation of unions and the destruction of collective bargaining. If the worker is given only the alternatives of industrial autocracy or the destruction of capitalism he will take his chances on a new order. This much is certain. There must be a full opportunity for free collective bargaining if capitalism is to survive. The realistic alternatives facing the democratic industrial society are to make collective bargaining work or to give way to the police state.

Make collective bargaining work. Ensure the success of industrial self-government or face the loss of our traditional freedoms. That is the challenge of an advancing technology, to labor, to management. Well, what does self-government demand from labor, from management, if it is to work? This book has attempted to give a few of the answers. It has suggested an industrial relations philosophy with management accepting the concept of democracy in industry and labor accepting the concept of full productivity.

Labor and management owe it to America to develop patterns of living together. They cannot use their power—power derived from the grant to associate and incorporate—to tear the economy apart. After all, the right of association, whether into corporations or unions, is a right granted to individuals by their government. This right carries with it a social responsibility. And it is government's duty to enforce that social responsibility. To the extent that these associations accept their public obligations, government can stay out of their affairs. Where the group does not practice public responsibility, it leaves government with no alternative but to step in and regulate or destroy the group.

Our economy, to remain liberal, must continue to grant the right of freedom of association, but it must, at the same time, insist that autonomous economic groups frankly assume social responsibility. And it must do this without destroying the group itself. It is one of the primary problems of modern, democratic government to fold these great interest-groupings into the economic and political structure of a free society without destroying either group or individual rights. This is the great, long-term problem raised by the growth of the corporation and the union. To date, we are apparently faced with the choice between self-restraint by the power blocs (self-government) or a dangerous extension of governmental power (the police state).

To serve themselves best, management and unions must recognize their mutual interdependence and their responsibility to the community. This is the great imperative of our time. It isn't a question of lip service to social idealism. It is a question of down-to-brass-tacks appraisal of our economic necessities.

We know that isolationism can be dangerous in an interdependent world. We are learning that isolationist conduct by any one group in our modern society is dangerous to our interdependent, interwoven economy. There is no better place to begin to end economic isolationism than in the collective bargaining process.

We have it in our power to move on to new heights of mental and material well-being. Or, we can go down as other civilizations have before us, because we were caught in the trap of an advancing technology which produced problems of living together which we could not solve.

Either we will make collective bargaining work or we will give way to the police state.

EYE TO EYE

"Eye to Eye" is the name of a pamphlet which was distributed by the Union-Management Committee on Incentives of the Doehler-Jarvis Corporation. The pamphlet was a part of an over-all plan to put incentives on a sound basis and to introduce the Time-study Steward system.

The pamphlet opens with letters from the union and the company. Charles Pack, president of the Doehler Company, wrote:

I earnestly recommend that this booklet be read by every Doehler worker. It will give you a clear understanding of the aims of the Doehler Company and of your Union in the field of cooperative time study.

An incentive system that will be simple and understandable and will be fair to the worker and to the Company is highly desirable. This booklet outlines such a system which has been developed jointly by representatives of your union and the company, under the guidance of a group of consulting engineers.

The company can only survive on the basis of efficiency. The worker wants, and should have, a fair standard of work. The plan outlined in this booklet aims to accomplish both of these objectives.

This plan represents an honest approach by the Company and the Union to the solution of a problem that has been a source of annoyance and dissatisfaction to the Company, the Union, and the workers, and it constitutes another milestone in the history of constructive labor-management relations that has existed, between your Company and your Union.

Edward T. Cheyfitz, at that time National Chairman of the CIO's Casting Division of the Mine, Mill and Smelter Workers' Union, wrote for the union:

> The publication of this booklet by the Doehler Incentive Committee is a forward step. Your reading and studying it will help you improve your standard of living, improve your relationship with your management, and contribute to the nation's welfare by increasing plant productivity.
>
> What are the objectives of the plan projected in this booklet? Well firstly, it provides an accurate method of measuring a normal or fair day's work. Secondly, it clearly separates the amount of work to be performed per hour and the amount of money to be paid per hour. Fair Time and Fair Payment are not dependent upon each other. And thirdly, the plan provides for Union Time-study Stewards. Here is an opportunity for the Union to have its own elected policemen to guarantee maintenance of agreed upon rules in Time-study Application.
>
> The adoption of this Elemental Standards system with Union Time-study Stewards will provide lasting benefits, including the elimination of a major source of Management-Labor conflict.

The text of the pamphlet follows.

FACTORIES, INCENTIVES, AND TIME STUDY

At the beginning of the war, Herb was the owner of a small garage well equipped with machinery for the repair of "anything which has wheels," as he put it.

The war put a big dent in his business, with gasoline rationing and everything, and even after laying off his two mechanic-helpers, he found that he was beginning to be idle himself. This worried Herb, for he still had to pay his rent, he still had to pay for his groceries, and the kids still had to have new clothes.

But one day a stranger came in, noticed an engine lathe in one corner, and asked Herb if he could spare some time to do a little lathe work for him. Herb, thinking it was just another odd job, told him he could if he would furnish the material.

Well, the man, Mr. Young, showed Herb a sample of the part and also a print, and told him he wanted ten pieces made. He also told him how much he would pay for them. Herb took one good look and sized the job up as "duck soup" at that price. The material was delivered the next day and a few days later the job was finished. It met Mr. Young's inspection requirements and Herb received his check. He was very happy about the deal.

A few days later Mr. Young dropped in again along with another man. This time they wanted Herb to make one hundred pieces of the same part that he had made on the order for ten. But they told Herb that this time he would have to furnish the material and that they would have to have a quotation from him before they could consider giving the large order.

Now naturally Herb wanted the business. So he told the men he would figure on the job and let them know what his price would be. And so he started figuring what his actual costs would be. He set his estimates down this way:

```
Labor: 400 hours @ $1...........................  $400
Material..........................................   165
Light, heat, rent, power, machinery replacement
    (overhead) ..................................   250
                                                  ----
    Total.........................................  $815
```

To be on the safe side, he gave them a figure of $915. They told him that the order was his and that he should go to work.

Which he did. Sensing that maybe more orders would be forthcoming if he delivered the work ahead of schedule, he hired one of his friends who knew how to run a lathe to work in the evenings. He paid the friend $1 an hour.

The friend hadn't worked many evenings until Herb saw that this chap couldn't turn out as much work per hour as he could.

To make a long story short, the order was finished and the final check came through. Being anxious to know how he stood, Herb again wrote down his actual cost figures to see how they looked compared with the estimate he had made.

	Estimate	Actual
Labor................................	$400	$480
Material.............................	165	185
Light, heat, rent, power, machinery replacement........................	250	250
Total............................	$815	$915

When Herb saw $915 as actual cost he was fighting mad. For all his worry and planning he had not made anything on the job. He had barely broken even. But having somewhat of a business head on him, he started to analyze the reasons why.

He saw the cost of his (and his helper's) labor was 20 per cent above estimate. That might be accounted for by Joe's not working so fast as he did and the fact that they had had some tool trouble. His material ran over his estimate because he had run more scrap on this order than on the other one. It was a tough lesson.

But Mr. Young was satisfied with the work and especially pleased because Herb had been able to deliver ahead of schedule. He told Herb that he would have more jobs for him if he wanted them. This put Herb up to a hard problem: he had to be sure his price would be neither too high nor too low.

Therefore, he went to a friend to ask his advice. This friend, Mr. Blake, was a production manager of one of the local factories. Together they went over the figures on the job just finished. In the end Mr. Blake summed up the situation like this:

"Herb, this may seem like a tough break to you, but it is a blessing in disguise. Remember, you didn't lose your shirt as many men just starting a business do. But the big point is that you now are willing to do something about it, not just blunder along.

"The fact is plain that you lost most of your profit on your incorrect estimate of the number of pieces you could turn out per hour.

"Now. You have learned two facts from your experience:

1. Not all men give the same performance, that is, do the same amount of work, per hour on the job, even though conditions are the same.
2. If you are going to stay in the business where you bid on a job, and then get that job to do at your own figure, you will have to know how to estimate accurately your labor costs. (Overhead and material estimating are not so difficult.)"

"How do other companies which are successful get around these problems?" asked Herb.

"Well," replied Mr. Blake, "to estimate and compute overhead and material cost they employ cost accountants. Every successful firm has a detailed cost-control system. To estimate and compute labor cost they employ Time-study Engineers. You have heard about them. They clock the jobs running in the plant and apply speed ratings to see how long it takes for the average operator to do them.

"After they have taken a large number of time studies, tables are built which tell how long it takes to do certain classes of jobs. Knowing this, the company can estimate pretty closely what it will cost to make any given number of parts which a customer wishes made.

"Other companies carry the process somewhat farther and build what are known as Elemental Production Standards. *But the purpose of all the various ways time studies are made is to give management an accurate yardstick by which it can estimate how long it will take to make a product, and hence how much they should ask for it from the customer.*

"No manufacturing business can exist long if it does not use some time study; guessing leads it to the same problem you have experienced.

"Perhaps you have had the feeling that time study is not necessary unless the plant is either on a flat piece-work plan or on an incentive plan. If you have, you have been wrong. *Whether you have an incentive plan or not, management of the company must have accurate time standards in order to accurately figure its selling price.*

"Remember, Herb, you had better know pretty accurately how much *time* will have to go into a product—or you will not stay in business long."

THE BEST TIME-STUDY SYSTEM

For a minute both Herb and Mr. Blake sat quietly. It was apparent Herb was doing some deep thinking. Then he spoke up.

"Time study is necessary. I must know how much work the average man will do on a job if he works at an average speed. I must have production standards if I want to stay in business. If you have time, I'd appreciate your telling me more about them. For instance, what different kinds of standards are there?"

"Briefly, there are two major kinds of production standards, Herb," Mr. Blake went on. "The first kind is known as the *job standard.*

"A job standard is one which is set by observing just one job—that operation to which it will apply. Many times the Time-study Observer will time the operation just once, then make his calculations and set the standard for it. Thus for every new part or every operation on a part, at least one study must be made.

"There are several shortcomings in job standards. Everything depends upon the quality of one, or maybe two observations. If the speed rating or 'leveling' is wrong, there is no chance to catch the mistake and the standard is in error. There is no check for consistency. One other characteristic makes job standards undesirable: there can be no rate set until the job has been timed.

"The second kind of production standard is the *elemental data standard*.

"This type gets it name from the fact that separate standards are actually set for each element which goes into the operation."

"But what are the elements?" asked Herb.

"Elements are each of the little pieces of work which make up an operation as it is listed on the operations sheets. A typical list of elements in die casting might be

"FIRST ELEMENT: Close die, get ladle, pour

"SECOND ELEMENT: Make shot, return ladle . . . die opens

"THIRD ELEMENT: Eject piece, piece to table

"FOURTH ELEMENT: Blow out die (die slick)

"FIFTH ELEMENT: Move to 'Close' position

"Another example, in the cleaning of die castings, might be

"FIRST ELEMENT: Pick up piece (from tote pan, on bench), transport to fixture (on bench, 2 ft.)

"SECOND ELEMENT: Secure piece in fixture (1 lever camlock)

"THIRD ELEMENT: File off gate ($\frac{1}{8}'' \times \frac{1}{8} \times 1''$) (12'' mill file)

"FOURTH ELEMENT: Release clamp, remove piece to tote pan (2 ft. on bench)

"FIFTH ELEMENT: Move to obtain new piece

"All these little operations—'Close die, get ladle, pour' or 'Secure piece in fixture'—are elements. By definition, then, an element is one or more work motions always performed in the same way.

"Elemental standards are, therefore, nothing more than production standards set for each of the elements on a scheduled operation."

Herb interrupted, "I can see how you would be able to time a complete operation or job, but how can you time these little operations or *elements?*"

"Just like you time complete operations, or cycles, as they are more properly called.   Except that you use a stop watch that has very fine divisions of a minute—either seconds or hundredths of a minute. The time-study observer does not stop the watch after he starts the study: he records the watch readings for each element, just as that element is finished. Continuous watch readings have the advantage of showing all the work and all the delays which went into the performance as the time-study man observed it being done.

"Now.   Remember your helper couldn't get out so many pieces in a given amount of time as you could. To get around this difficulty most time-study men 'level' or 'speed-rate' their observed elements.   That is, they mark down their idea of the performance given by the operator they are observing.   This is necessary to prevent standards being set in terms of the very skillful or very fast man, or to prevent the standards being set on the unskillful or slow man. Either case would be wrong. You must set your standard for the 'average' man giving an 'average' or 'normal' performance.   Leveling helps accomplish this.

"A normal performance is that pace which a normal experienced operator can maintain for the entire work period without acquiring undue fatigue, assuming he is given his usual necessary allowances—the personal factor, including fatigue.

"Take for example the case of a man doing a 'File off gate' element. He was observed to have averaged 0.15 minute. But the observer knew he was working faster than the 'average' man by 20 per cent. Therefore he leveled him at 120 per cent. Hence the element standard should be 0.15×120 per cent, or 0.18 minute. This is the standard time in which the average man will do this element on this kind of a job, and under these same conditions.

"From this you can see that by setting standards on all the elements which would occur in an operation, we can get the total operation standard by adding up the normalized time values for all its elements."

"Is it really as simple as that?" asked Herb.

"No, actually there are many safeguards put in to be sure the element standards are right.

"Under the elemental data method, the time-study department will check each study for consistency within the study itself, and also for consistency with the time taken for the same identical elements on many other studies which have been made. This is done by using thoroughly tested and accepted scientific statistical methods.

"Many, many studies are taken to build up the curves, charts, and tables from which the standards are actually set. These techniques of treatment assure getting the time required for the performance of an element by the 'average' man."

"What are the advantages of the elemental data method?" asked Herb.

"You might list them as follows," replied Mr. Blake.

1. Elemental Production standards are accurately set for the *average* operator. All employees agree that they want to do a normal day's work—they call it a fair day's work. This is what management expects of them. This method sets all standards for the 'average' man.

2. The Elemental Data method allows the standard to be set before the job goes on the floor. Hence from the beginning the operator knows what is expected of him. Thus the Elemental Data method is the best available general method for defining the 'task' for an operator.

3. The Elemental Data method gives management the best tools available for estimating and pricing, scheduling, costing, etc.

4. The Elemental Data method will eliminate arguments on what is 'normal' performance for each individual job.   It sets as accurately as possible a 'fair' day's work.   The worker appreciates this protection given to his interests."

Herb reflected for a moment, then got up, thanked Mr. Blake for his help, and departed for home.

THE "TIME" AUDITOR—THE UNION TIME-STUDY STEWARD

Battleships, concrete mixers, bobby pins, battery boxes—they all take *time* to build.   Measurement of time is so important to industry that a manufacturing plant cannot stay in business unless it measures its usable time.

But *time* is the one thing a worker has to sell.   The manufacturer pays the worker for his *time*.   If the worker is not active during the time he sells to the employer, if he does not produce, the employer does not get the value he should for the money he pays to the employee.   On the other hand, if the employee works harder or faster than "normal," he doesn't get what he should for his time—unless the employer pays him for the extra work above the "normal" through some sort of an incentive pay plan.

Therefore, it is much to the interest of both worker and employer to know exactly how much time it should take a normal or "average," experienced employee, working at an "average" pace, to do a piece of work under a given set of conditions.   The manufacturer hires time-study men to get this information for him.   The manufacturer uses this information to figure his plant schedules, his costs, his selling prices.

But to see that the company doesn't make mistakes in figuring what an "average" employee should do on a particular job in a given length of time, the union is now using . . .

The Union Time-study Steward.—The office of union time-study steward has been created in a number of companies to give the worker someone from within the Union who is qualified to pass judgment on production standards which are in effect. The position of the time-study steward is somewhat similar to that of an auditor or accountant who may be engaged by the union to look at the company books when wage questions arise. However, the union time-study steward is available at all times.

Duties of the Time-study Steward.—The union time-study steward has only one major function. He reviews any and all production standards which any pieceworker sincerely feels are out of line. He is responsible to the Union for the discharge of that duty through the Stewards and Officers Council, to which body he reports once a month. He will fall under the administration of one of the division superintendents on such matters as hours worked, vacations, pay deductions, bonds, etc.

In the discharge of his duty of reviewing questioned production standards, he will

1. Check the job to see whether it is running to "standard conditions"; *i.e.*, whether it is running under the same conditions as when it was timed and under the conditions as specified by the operation sheet

2. Check the standard to see that it includes all necessary elements

3. Check the standard to see that it includes all the usual and necessary allowances

4. Check the calculation of the standard to see that no mistake has been made in figuring it

5. Present an explanation of his findings to the operator who requested the check, and a written report to the time-study engineer

If a time-study steward has passed his opinion on a complaint and the operator still feels that he has a case of protest, he has the privilege of filing a grievance in the usual manner.

If the time-study engineer fails to agree with a decision written by the time-study steward, he has the privilege of asking that the decision be reviewed by a review board composed of the following:

> The time-study steward who has handled the complaint
> The time-study engineer
> A competent impartial person

During the course of the collection of elemental data, it is the duty of the time-study steward to keep posted on the progress of the program, the accuracy and the adequacy of the data, the fixing of allowances, and the preparation of tables of elemental production standards with their application procedures.

There will be no designation as to where a time-study steward will work.   Time-study stewards will be trained to work in all departments of the plant.

Selection of the Time-study Stewards.—From the above, the fact is apparent that the union time-study steward must be a very able man or woman. He must be able to deal intelligently and impartially with the problems which he encounters. He must be able to understand the techniques used by time-study engineer, analyst, and observer. He must be acquainted with all the processes which are carried on in the shop and must have an adequate technical vocabulary. He must be interested in learning more about the problems of both management and labor. He must be able to handle arithmetic problems with ease. Above all *he must have the courage to be honest and to " call them the way he sees them."* These are some of the qualities which the time-study steward must have to serve the workers of this plant most effectively.

To ensure the selection of the persons best fitted for this work, a psychologist from the staff of Stevenson, Jordan & Harrison will interview nine candidates, finally choosing the three who are best suited for the position.   These *candidates will be elected* by their respective departments as follows:

> Four (4) from cleaning department
> Three (3) from the casting department, and
> Two (2) from the foundry

From these nine candidates, the psychologist will make his selection; however, one must come from the cleaning department and one from the casting or foundry; the third may come from any one of these three departments.

Length of Term of the Time-study Steward.—The term of the time-study steward shall be three (3) years.   When a term expires, the same general procedure will be followed for the selection of another time-study steward as was used for the first appointment.   However, this time all production departments as a whole will elect four (4) candidates. If the incumbent time-study steward is elected as one of the four candidates, he will automatically continue in office for the next term.

To ensure there always being at least one trained and experienced time-study steward in service, the terms of the three time-study stewards will be staggered or overlapped. Therefore, one new time-study steward will be elected each 12 months.   This is the same procedure now used in electing local union trustees.   For the first group this means that there will be one 12-month term, one 24-month term, and one full term (three years.)   After the training is completed, the individual who will fill the short term, the intermediate term, and the long term will be decided by drawing lots.

Should either the Management or the Union be dissatisfied with the efforts of a time-study steward, he or she can be removed by a majority ruling of a board consisting of the following:

> The time-study steward who has the greatest or next greatest seniority as a time-study steward

The union president
The time-study engineer
The time-study analyst
A competent impartial person

A complaint for removal can be drawn only by or through the union president or the time-study engineer. A dated copy of this complaint must be filed with each member of the board. Hearing of the complaint will be set for two weeks after the date the complaint was filed. Any complaint can be withdrawn in this period by the person (union president or time-study engineer) who filed it. A decision must be reached and made effective by this board within a period not longer than two weeks after its first meeting of consideration of the case. The judgment of this board is final.

Pay Rate of the Time-study Steward.—The hourly rate of the time-study steward will be determined by job evaluation. He will accumulate seniority during his service, and upon termination of his services as time-study steward and his return to production, he will be automatically reinstated to the seniority unit from which he came.

Training of the Union Time-study Steward.—After selection, the three time-study stewards will be trained in the methods of elemental production standards along with as many trainees as the company wishes to appoint. This is essential to assure consistency of viewpoint and application of methods.

Briefly the material covered by the training program will include:

1. The reasons for Time Study
2. The functions of the Time-study Department
3. The responsibilities of the Time-study Observer, the Analyst, and the Engineer
4. The functions and responsibilities of the Time-study Steward
5. How to make well defined, accurate stop-watch time studies

6. Development of speed and accuracy in making watch readings and in making cycle and element ratings

7. Blueprint reading along with development of ability to make accurate work sketches

8. Mathematics necessary to the solution of shop problems, and to the computing of time standards

9. Time-study and trade terminology

10. Development of a broad knowledge of and acquaintance with machines and tooling used in the industry

11. Training in the planning of methods and processes

12. Development of the ability to level or rate observed performance

During the course of this training program continued emphasis will be given to practice in rating (speed rating, as it has been known formerly). The object of the continued practice is to be certain that both Time-study Stewards and Company time-study personnel have a common and crystal-clear concept of what "normal" performance is.

Using the Time-study Steward.—The office of Time-study Steward like any other good thing can be made to be very valuable to the workers of Doehler, or it can be reduced to a position of impotence, insignificance, and even fraud. The selection and use made of the time-study steward *by the workers* will determine the success with which this office can serve them. The time-study steward should be called in only when an operator sincerely feels the standard is not correctly set and is working an injustice on him. Then he is justified in asking the time-study steward for his opinion and, for that matter, should take this step. The operator should respect this opinion just as much as he would that of any well-trained expert in any field.

The tentative procedure for obtaining the service of the time-study steward is as follows:

The operator will have the departmental clerk fill out a Request for Check of Production Standard. This slip will either be picked up by the time-study steward or will be forwarded immediately to him. After the time-study steward investigates the problem he will present his findings to the operator and the time-study engineer, to the latter in writing (as outlined under Duties of the time-study steward). As proven by past experience, if the operator is wrong, the time-study steward will have little difficulty in demonstrating the fact to him. On the other hand, if the operator is right and a standard has been inadvertently set wrong, he, the time-study steward, will have little difficulty convincing the time-study engineer that an error has been made.

Remember, the union time-study steward and the men of the time-study department are going to be concerned with fact and fact alone—just as any other engineer would work, and as you would want them to work.

SIXTY-FOUR-DOLLAR QUESTIONS AND THEIR ANSWERS

1. What is the question on which the incentive workers of foundry, casting and cleaning departments will vote?

The incentive workers of the foundry, casting and cleaning departments will be asked to vote on the referendum only on this question:

Do you wish union time-study stewards, trained in the methods of time study, to represent you on production standards?

2. What is the advantage of the proposed new plan?

While the proposed new plan embraces several changes, the principal one, and the one on which the incentive workers will vote, is that it will provide for the training and the installation of union time-study stewards.

3. How will the presence of a union time-study steward be valuable to you as an operator?

The union time-study steward will be trained in time-study work. Hence he is in better position to make a presentation of your difficulties to the time-study department than you are. Furthermore, his sole duty is that of checking standards on which there are complaints. Not being busy with other difficulties, he can devote his full time to inquiring into them. Then too as a Union member he is concerned with exactly the same problems as you are.

4. How will the union time-study steward be valuable to the Union as a body?

He will provide the same kind of assurance to the Union that an auditor provides to the stockholders of a company. That is, the Union can be sure everything connected with time study and setting of standards will be "on the up-and-up." This plainly will lead to better labor relations for it builds confidence by determining whether or not the Time-study Department and the methods it uses are factual, unbiased, and "above board."

5. For whom will the union time-study stewards work?

So far as hours worked, vacations, etc., the union time-study steward will report to one of the division superintendents. Regarding his activities, he will be responsible to the local. On the quality of his work, the time-study steward will report to the Stewards and Officers Council. It should be clearly understood that the union time-study steward does not work for the time-study department. But he will work closely with the time-study department. He has access to all time-study records, charts, graphs, and other memoranda having to do with the setting of production standards.

6. Will the time-study steward help the time-study department in setting production standards?

Absolutely no. The time-study department sets all rates. The time-study steward is concerned with a rate only when a complaint is filed on it.

7. Will the time-study steward be present when studies are being made by the time-study observer?

He may or may not be present when a time study is being taken by one of the time-study observers. The time-study steward has no authority over the time-study observer;

if he has any complaints on the ways the studies are being taken, he will present these complaints to the time-study engineer.

8. After a complaint is filed with the time-study steward, how long will it be before he looks into the difficulty?

He will review the complaint as soon as he can get to it. He will review all complaints in the order in which he receives them.

9. Does one have to have a lot of schooling to be eligible for selection as a time-study steward?

Definitely no. The past experience of Stevenson, Jordan & Harrison indicates that many men who have not had a lot of formal schooling have made excellent time-study stewards. Remember that there are many other characteristics besides formal education which are important on this job: the ability to get along with your fellow workers is very essential; the amount of backbone you have; your disposition to be truthful regardless of what others think of you; and your ability to think in terms of fact and not in terms of fancy. These are as important as formal education—maybe more so. From a practical viewpoint, however, a grammar-school education is necessary.

10. Will the time-study steward have anything to do with earnings?

No. The time-study steward will be concerned *only* with the correctness of the production standard in terms of time. If employees feel they are not getting enough money for the job they are doing, and if the production standard is right, it becomes a case for negotiation between the union and management.

11. Will the new time-study system be placed in effect in all three departments (cleaning, casting, and foundry) at the same time?

No. The plan will be installed in these departments in the following order: (1) the cleaning department; (2) the casting department; and (3) the foundry.

The union time-study stewards will not function in a

department until that department is working on the new standards. That the time-study steward will serve in any department wherever needed should be clearly understood. He is not assigned to any one department.

12. What effect will the new system have on earnings on new jobs coming into the plant?

The intention of both the company and the union is that this modification of method of time study shall result in equalized earnings for equal performances. It is not the intention of the company or the union that the new plan shall increase or reduce the earnings of the operators.

13. Will the basic rates now being used in computation of piece rates be changed?

Present basic rates are actually computation rates. They will be changed to the new computation rates based on the ratio between the present and the new concepts of normal performance. Hourly guaranteed rates for samples, adjustments, and other existing rates for special conditions, are subject to collective bargaining, and are not affected by this plan.

14. Will any of the present rates be reduced as a result of the installation of this new system?

Management has always guaranteed that rates will not be cut (for the same work). Management still holds to this principle. The installation of the new plan may disclose some "gravy" jobs. Management and the union know "gravy" jobs create dissatisfaction in the department and undermine the wage structure, benefiting only a few. Even in the face of this, management states, it will continue the present piecework rates on all current or old jobs, until the union decides they shall be corrected.

If on the other hand, the installation indicates that the production standards have been too tight, they will be adjusted upward, giving the operator proportionally increased earnings.

15. Why do both the company and the union recommend a change in the time-study system now being used?

Briefly, the union wants to be certain that the company does not except more than a fair day's work for a fair day's pay.

The company wants to know that its standards are correct in order to accurately determine costs, estimate selling prices, and plan and control production within the shop.

Both management and the union want a system which will provide the same yardstick for measuring performance everywhere in the shop. They both want this yardstick to express "task" in terms of what the normal experienced man can be rightfully expected to do. The elemental data method provides such a yardstick. Hence it is desired by both management and the union. For work beyond "normal performance," pay will be increased by incentive payments the same as at the present time.

16. What is the elemental data method?

Briefly, the elemental data method provides for the setting of production standards by breaking the operations into clearly defined "elements." Many, many time studies (on these elements) are taken and then leveled or normalized to convert them to "normal" time. These normalized element times are scientifically compared with previously collected normalized element times (for the same class of work) to get a standard which is "average" for the element.

An operation standard is obtained by adding up the element standards for each of the elements necessary in that operation.

17. How can the operator be sure that the idea of "normal performance," which is used as the measuring stick of the operator's performance, is right?

Under the supervision of the instructor, the time-study trainees, both company and union, will be trained so that they both have the same concept of "normal performance." They will be given much practice in evaluating performance on the floor in terms of this normal. Thus, if the union time-study steward agrees with the concept which he is taught the operator should not have any doubts about it.

Furthermore, the many studies taken on the same elements by several time-study observers will show up any glaring differences in rating when these element times are scientifically checked against each other.

18. What is a production or operation standard?

A production or operation standard is the average time required to perform a given operation using specified tools, equipment, and materials in a specified manner, by an experienced operator working with normal or average skill and effort, and including the proper time allowances.

19. Will the elemental data method produce standards which are in favor of the company? Will they be in favor of the operator?

In either case the answer is NO! This system sets standards in terms of the "average experienced operator," which is in favor of nobody. It is purely an impartial standard.

20. Will provision be made for putting necessary allowances into the standard?

Yes. Provision will be made for including necessary extra time allowances in the standards. Such allowances might be for personal needs, for rest (fatigue), or for other miscellaneous delays such as oiling ejector pins or changing lathe tools.

21. How will allowances be determined?

Necessary extra allowances will be determined by the same general methods used for the establishing of elemental standards. That is, many instances of their occurrence will be timed. By seeing how often a particular delay repeats itself, and by observing its time, we can establish very closely how often it will happen on future operations of a particular kind, and how long it will take. We can then add these time values into the elemental values to get our elemental standards.

Establishing proper fatigue allowances will be a rather

complicated matter. Until that subject is investigated, fatigue allowances will be made in much the same manner as they are at present.

22. Does the standard include everything the operator *must* do?

Yes. If it is necessary for the operator to go to the tool crib, to move a tote box, or to oil ejector pins—in short, all those activities which are necessary to the job will be included in the standard.

23. Will the elemental standards method compensate the operator for difficulties such as faulty dies, dull tools, etc?

Yes. Standard conditions, the conditions which are specified for the performance of the operation, assume that tools are working properly. If the conditions require that the operator put in extra work, or take more time than allowed under standard conditions, allowances will be made to cover this amount of time. Such allowances will be determined by the time-study department.

24. Will each job have to be *time studied* when it goes on the floor?

No. Because production standards are to be built up from tables of elemental time values, many standards can be set without having actually to time the jobs on the floor. It will, however, be necessary to observe the job to be certain its contents are proper. This is an advantage to both the operator and the company for it makes certain even short run jobs will be covered by standards.

Until the elemental production tables are complete, jobs will have to be timed just as they are at present.

25. Will a time-study man time a job before it is running to standard conditions?

He may. Remember, under elemental standards, no production standard is set directly from any one time study which is made. Even though there may be some elements that are not right, the time-study observer may take a study of an operation to gather data on those elements which are all right.

26. How many studies will be made on a job?

As many as the time-study analyst thinks are desirable. Under the elemental data method, the objective is to build standards from average figures. Therefore, to have average data, one must take more than one study. Regardless of the number of studies made on a particular job, the standard is not set from any one of these observations; it is set from data which is collected from many different jobs. The operator should welcome more than one observation for it assures him that average data are being used.

27. Will there be a maximum or minimum "speed" or "performance" rating?

From now on we shall use the term "performance rating" instead of "speed rating," because it better describes what is done when elements or cycles are rated. There is no theoretical limit, up or down to the leveling or rating factors which may be used; the rating given all depends upon the speed and skill of the operator while he is being observed.

28. Will there be a prescribed number of minutes a job must be time studied?

No. The observer continues his observation and time recordings until he is certain that he has seen virtually all there is in the job. That is, he will have a record of practically all the "non-cyclic" work involved in the operation as well as a very good record of the "cyclic" elements. It might be that he will stay with the job for a full shift; or again he might get the complete picture in half an hour. He will be trained in how to determine how long to continue observations.

29. Will the time-study observer who takes the studies on the floor actually set the rates as in the past?

No, the standard will be set by the time-study engineer using his tables of elemental production standards which correspond to the specifications of the job and the methods which are specified for it on the operation sheet.

30. Will down time count against the operator's efficiency?

No. Whenever an operator is "down," through no fault of his own, he will be paid his "down-time" rate just as he is at present.

31. If an operator is required to set up his own job, will that time be counted into the production time?

No. If an operator sets his own job, he will be given time to do that work. His efficiency will be calculated only on the time he is on production.

32. If an operation is done on either of two different kinds of machines, will the same standard be used for both?

No. If the production conditions are different, the standard must be set for each different situation. It is conceivable that although a standard is set for two different machines or situations it might be the same for both, but this is unlikely.

33. What happens when an operation is not set up according to the operation sheet?

Quite likely a temporary standard will be set. As soon as the operation is running "to standard" the proper time standard will be applied.

34. Does the same standard apply to both men and women when either may work on the job?

Yes. When the production standards are set, standard time requirements are based on either sex doing the work.

35. Will the same production standards apply to all individuals?

Yes. The standard is set for the "average" operator. It will remain the same for all who work on the operation involved.

36. Under what conditions will the company have the right to change standards?

Management will have the right to change standards under the following conditions:

(*a*) If a clerical error is discovered in the standard which has been set.

(*b*) If a measurable time difference occurs because of changes (such as changes in die, the substitution of a new die, changes in tools, setup, methods, materials, machines or equipment) which are made. Obviously the whole cycle will have to be checked to discover the effect on the elemental composition of the cycle.

A "measurable time difference" will be defined as a 5 per cent increase or decrease in any one change, or 7 per cent for cumulative changes.

If an operator submits mechanical improvements which make greater production possible (and which are accepted by the company) management will find other means of compensating the originator of the idea. The details of compensation are being worked out and will be submitted to the Union.

37. What happens to an operation standard if inspection standards are changed?

The operation will be retimed and the operation standard will be changed to conform to the new requirements.

38. Will it be necessary to retime all jobs in the shop when the new time-study system is put into effect?

Yes. It will be necessary to retime all direct labor operations in the shop to be certain that all production standards are on the same basis. In other words, both the company and the union are anxious that equal effort and skill (performance) result in equal pay, everywhere in the shop for any particular type of work.

CHARTER OF THE TOLEDO LABOR-MANAGEMENT-CITIZENS COMMITTEE

Industrial harmony is necessary to the welfare of Toledo. Industrial harmony means more than the elimination of strikes, slowdowns, and lockouts. It means a practical, common-sense recognition of the rights of both employers and employees, the mutuality of their interests, and the importance of their joint responsibility to the citizens as a whole, whose interests transcend the presumed rights of any group.

To jointly seek successful patterns of democratic economic living and to achieve self-government in industry, and to provide a means of minimizing and reducing the possibility of loss of production and wages, this Industrial Relations Charter has been drafted and is recommended for consideration and adoption by representatives of Industry and Labor in the City of Toledo.

PRINCIPLE NO. 1

Management acknowledges the right of employees to form and join labor organizations without interference or coercion from any source, and to bargain collectively through their bargaining agents. For their part, bargaining agents recognize their duty to demonstrate leadership and responsibility in keeping with the trust reposed in them.

PRINCIPLE NO. 2

Labor recognizes the inherent right of Management to direct the operations of the enterprise. In the exercise of these rights, Management recognizes its duty to demonstrate the type of leadership and responsibility it expects of the representatives of Labor under Principle No. 1.

PRINCIPLE NO. 3

Neither Labor nor Management should discriminate against any employee because of race, creed or color.

PRINCIPLE NO. 4

Management and Labor agree that improvements in productive efficiency and technological advances result in lower costs and selling prices and wider markets for the products of industry, thereby making possible higher wages and a rising standard of living and increasing employment.

PRINCIPLE NO. 5

Management and Labor, while attempting to prevent differences and disagreements, realize that they will arise from time to time, and believe that the damaging effects of such differences and disagreements on the community should be minimized by joint discussion and by the voluntary utilization of mediation, fact-finding, and arbitration facilities as may be made available by this Labor-Management-Citizens Committee.

PRINCIPLE NO. 6

Managemnet and Labor agree that an educational program is desirable to promote a better mutual understanding between workers, stewards, union officials, supervisors, foremen, and managers. As a means to that end, an educational program shall be organized as an essential activity of this Labor-Management-Citizens Committee.

ARTICLE NO. 1

There shall be created a Labor-Management-Citizens Committee of eighteen (18) persons to be appointed by the Mayor of the City of Toledo, to act as a directing body for the purpose of implementing and effectuating the purposes and principles of this Charter and the amendments thereto.

ARTICLE NO. 2

The Committee shall consist of six recognized members from Labor, six recognized members from Industry, and six representatives from the Public. The members shall be appointed for a term of one year. The Mayor shall designate one of the Public members to act as Chairman.

ARTICLE NO. 3

The Committee shall adopt a set of rules to govern its own meetings and procedure. These rules may be amended from time to time, but only upon notice to all members that said proposed amendments shall be acted upon at a specified meeting. A majority vote of the Committee shall be required for the approval of the proposed amendment.

ARTICLE NO. 4

The Committee may appoint an Executive Secretary who may be a full-time employee.

ARTICLE NO. 5

There may be created an Office of Mediation, Fact Finding, and Arbitration. The facilities of the Office of Mediation, Fact Finding, and Arbitration shall be available on joint application of the parties to a difference or disagreement. In any matter that is to be arbitrated, there shall be a stipulation signed by both parties clearly defining the issue or issues to be decided and a statement to the effect that the decision will be accepted by both parties as final and binding.

ARTICLE NO. 6

A Budget shall be annually prepared by the Committee in the month of November for the ensuing year, the funds to be supplied by the City.

ARTICLE NO. 7

The Director of the Office of Mediation, Fact Finding, and Arbitration shall be appointed by unanimous vote of the Committee for a period of two (2) years; provided, however, that should objection to him be lodged with the Committee within six months of his appointment, a hearing shall be held by said Committee. If a majority of the Committee should decide that the objections are well taken, his resignation shall be accepted. Provisions for such resignation procedure shall be made in the contract. After the six months' period, the Director of the Office of Mediation, Fact Finding, and Arbitration shall serve the full two years unless removed for fraud or misfeasance in office.

ARTICLE NO. 8

The Office of Mediation, Fact Finding, and Arbitration shall submit its rules of procedure for approval by the Committee. Such approval to be by unanimous vote of the Committee.

ARTICLE NO. 9

Whenever it comes to the attention of the Office of Mediation, Fact Finding, and Arbitration that a Labor-Management dispute exists that may adversely affect the welfare of the community, and the parties to the dispute have not jointly requested the mediation or arbitration facilities available, the Director shall notify the Chairman of the Committee. The Chairman of the Committee, at his discretion, shall thereupon call a meeting of the Committee and/or request one or more Management members of the Committee to confer with the employer-disputant, and one or more Labor members of the Committee to confer with the representatives of the employees-disputant, and acquaint both parties to the dispute with the mediation and arbitration facilities available to them.

ARTICLE NO. 10

Should a jurisdictional dispute occur that may adversely affect the welfare of the community, the Committee shall make such recommendations it deems necessary.

ARTICLE NO. 11

The Charter shall become effective on the date that it is ratified by the Council of the City of Toledo. Amendments to this Charter shall come into effect when approved by a unanimous vote of the Committee. All proposed amendments must be presented in writing and lie over for thirty days before being considered. In the event that the Committee feels that an emergency exists, the Article requiring the proposed amendment to lie over 30 days may, by unanimous vote of the Committee, be suspended and the matter taken up for immediate consideration.

ARTICLE NO. 12

The parties to this Charter shall be those Management and Union groups in this community who shall make a separate or joint application for a certificate setting forth their endorsement of the Principles, Articles and Objectives of this Charter. This certificate shall remain in the possession of the applicant for this certificate so long as the provisions contained therein are adhered to. A certificate of participation may be issued or revoked by a majority vote of the Committee.

Ratified Feb. 5, 1946

Judge Frank L. Kloeb,
United States District Court

Rev. Michael J. Doyle,
Director of the Toledo Catholic Charities

Rev. F. Bringle McIntosh,
Dist. Superintendent of Methodist Churches

C. K. Searles,
Dean, College of Business Administration, University of Toledo

Rabbi Morton Goldberg,
B'Nai Israel Synagogue

Jules D. Lippman,
President, Chamber of Commerce

Preston Levis,
President, Owens-Illinois Glass Company

John D. Biggers,
President, Libbey-Owens-Ford Glass Company

Royce Martin,
President, Electric Auto-Lite Company

Joseph L. Tillman,
Vice-President, Unitcast Corporation

A. *Gideon Spieker,*
  Secretary-Treasurer
    Henry J. Spieker Company
Otto Brach
  Secretary, Toledo Central
  Labor Union, AFL
William Sturm,
  Regional Director, AFL
Franz Berlacher,
  Vice-President, Toledo
  Central Labor Union, AFL

Edward T. Cheyfitz,
  Chairman, Mine, Mill and
  Smelter Workers, CIO
Lawrence Steinberg,
  Ohio Director, Wholesale
  and Retail Clerks, CIO
Richard Gosser,
  Regional Director, UAW-
  CIO
Michael DiSalle,
  Vice-Mayor

INDEX

A

Acceptance of union, 6, 14, 50
Accurate work measurement, 57, 61
Agreement upon principles, 115, 118
Allis-Chalmers, 46
Aluminum Company of America, 46
American Bankers Association, 77
American Civil Liberties Union, 18
American Federation of Labor, 13,
   58, 77, 85, 112–114, 116–117
American Locomotive, 46
American Management Association,
   70
"America's Sixty Years' War," 13–
   14, 16
Arbitration, 40
Archer, T. P., 49
Armstrong Cork, 46
Associated Press, 111
Attlee, Clement, 98
Australia, 14

B

Barriers to imports, 77
Bath, Cyril, 45
Bedeaux, 25
Bendix, 46
Benton, William, 106
Blythe, H. E., 96
Boom-or-bust cycle, 105
Bracket wage payment, 85
British Cotton Textile Mission, 26
Business statesmanship, 103–104

C

Carter, Robert, 56
Casting Division, CIO, 51
Caterpillar Tractor, 46

Chamber of Commerce, U.S., 77,
   106, 115–116
Chemical Workers Union, AFL, 49
Chicago Virden Coal Company, 13
Christopher, George T., 67
Chrysler, 46
Cleveland, Grover, Commission on
   the Pullman Strike, 13–14
Closed shop, 28
Code of principles, 116
Collective bargaining, 32, 34, 40–42,
   44, 51, 53–54, 121
   constructive, 111, 117
Commerce, U.S. Department of, 93
Commission on the Causes of Indus-
   trial Unrest (1912), 13
Commission of Inquiry of the Inter-
   Church Movement on Steel
   Strike (1919), 13
Commission on the Pullman Strike,
   13–14
Committee for Economic Develop-
   ment, 77, 104
Commonwealth v. Hunt (Massa-
   chusetts), 14
Company policy, 32, 35
Conciliation Service of Department
   of Labor, 97, 98
CIO, 66, 77, 85, 112–114, 116–117
Cooperation, for efficiency, 51–52
   labor-management, 7, 45, 48
Cooperative planning, 51, 54
Corning Glass, 46

D

Deflated earnings, 73
Democracy, 2
   in industry, 115
   and production, 116–117
Democratic discipline, 17–18

Department of Agriculture, 90, 93
Department of Justice, 41
Department of Labor, 69
Detroit News, 112
Dictatorial discipline, 17
Dietz, Walter, 94
Discrimination in industry, 28–29
Dispute settlement, 35, 39, 109
Doehler-Jarvis Company, 51–54
Dooley, Channing, 94
Dynamics of Time Study (Presgrave), 62

E

Eargle, W. E., 71
Eastman Kodak, 46
Economic citizenship, 8
Economic democracy, 3
Economic dictatorship, 3
Economic interdependence, 119
Economic toll bridges, 104
Efficiency, improved, 47
    promotion of by government, 97–98
Efficiency advances, 48
Efficiency approaches, 51
Electrical Workers Union, CIO, 48
Elemental motions, 63
Employee attitudes, 42, 86
Employment in Manufacturing (1899–1939), 27
Employment, full, 26, 102–104, 106, 109–110
Employment policy, 28
England, 14
Expansionists, 104

F

Fair day's work, 57–58
Fair wage, 58
Farm-work simplification, 91–92
Feather-bedding, 22
Federal Home Loan Bank Board, 41
Ford Motor Company, 27
Foreign trade, 77
Foreman-steward relationship, 50–51

Fortune, 12
Freedom, of association, 122
    in industry, 16–17, 19
    in union, 18
Full employment, 26, 102–104, 106, 109–110

G

Gallup poll, 112
General Electric, 46
General Motors, 49, 75
Glass Bottle Blowers Association, 23
Golden, Clinton, 11
Goodyear Aircraft Corporation, 96
Goodyear Rubber, 46
Government, in business, 105
    and farmer, 90–91
Government policy, on industrial relations, 89
    on productivity, 99
Green, William, 115
Grievance machinery, 35, 39
Group living, 1
Group relationship, 14, 109
Growth of trade unions, 120

H

Hall, Max, 111
Hard, William, 41
Hearst newspapers, 111
High-level employment, 26
High-level productivity, 24, 28, 104
High-wage policy, 103
Hoffman, Paul, 106

I

Import barriers, 77
Incentive earnings, 55
Incentive plans, 22, 35, 87
Incentive rates, 55, 60, 69, 71
Incentive wage and economic isolation, 77
Incentives, 56, 70–78, 99
    acceptance of, 75
    opposition to, 74
    year of, by management, 72

Individual freedom, 14–17, 19
Individual performance, 84
Individuality in industry, 84, 86–88
Industrial citizenship, 11, 19
Industrial compulsion, 16
Industrial democracy, 121
Industrial dictatorship, 10, 17, 21
Industrial efficiency, 17, 22, 102
Industrial freedom, 17
Industrial peace, 102, 117
Industrial self-government, 3–9, 20, 42, 111, 121
Industrial warfare, 18, 117
Industrial waste, 22, 23, 25, 28
Industry, labor policy of, 8
Inflated earnings, 72
International Business Machines, 46
Isolationism, 123

J

Job description, 83
Job evaluation, 16, 80, 81–82, 84, 87, 97
Job measurement 82, 84
Job rating, 84
Job relationship, 80, 83
Job worth, 80, 82
Johns-Manville, 46
Johnston, Eric A., 115
Johnston-Murray-Green charter, 115–116, 118

L

Labor, Department of, Conciliation Service of, 97–98
Labor-Management News, 97
Labor-management production committees, 45–52, 97, 98
Labor, acceptance of productivity of, 30
    industrial relations policy of, 8
    living standard of, 30
    participation in policy making of, 38
LaFollette Senate Sub-Committee on Civil Liberties (1936–1940), 14

Larus and Brother, 47
Leadership through consent, 16
Libbey-Owens-Ford Glass Company, 43
Lincoln Electric Company, 71
Louisville Courier-Journal, 112
Lyon, Incorporated, 71

M

Magnuson, Senator Warren C., 99
Man-hour productivity, 22
Man-measurement yardstick, 86
Man rating, 84–85
Management, through compulsion, 37
    by consent, 37
    prerogatives of, 16, 20
    rights of, 20, 36–37
        usurpation of, 37
    techniques of, 16
Manager, role of, in full-employment economy, 103
Mass consumption, principle of, 103–104
Mass-pricing policy, 103
Mass production, 20, 101
Merit increases, 86
Merit rating, 16, 85–86, 89
Military Appropriations Act, 99
Monopoly power of unions, 107
Monsanto Chemical Company, 48–49, 53
Morrissey, Margaret Mary, 3
Murray Corporation, 63, 66
Murray, Phillip, 115

N

National Association of Manufacturers, 77, 106, 116
National Association State Chambers of Commerce, 96
National Bureau of Economic Research (1943), 27
National Cash Register, 46
National Farm Work Simplification Project, 91

National industrial relations policy, 5–6, 111
National Labor Relations Act (Wagner Act), 13–14, 89
New York Times, The, 112
Normalizing, 60
Normal performance, 61
Normal rating, 64
Normal work output per man per hour, 55
Normal-work yardstick, 59
North American Aviation, 46

O

Occupational ladder, 80–82

P

Packard Company, 67
Patterns of living together, 122
Payment, by hour, 70
  by result, 70–71
Personal freedom, 12
Personnel approach, 44
Personnel practices, sound, 42
Platt, Sir Frank, 26
Plomb Tool Company, 47
Politics of economics, 109
Presgrave, Ralph, 62
Production, plus democracy, 20, 36, 44
  with freedom, 6, 8, 19–20, 35–36, 38, 42, 52–53, 89, 100, 102, 106, 109, 111, 115–118
PMH (production per man-hour), 25–28, 30–31, 47, 69, 77, 88–89, 90, 94, 100
Production committees, 45–52, 97–98
Production pegging, 22, 24
Production restrictions, 22–23
Productive efficiency, 6
Productivity, acceptance of, 31, 50, 89
  and civilization, 29–30
  increase of, 26, 28, 31, 54, 70, 97, 117

Productivity, promotion by the government of, 90, 93, 98–99
  techniques of, 20–21
Price increases, 30
Profit drive, 5
Profit motive, 30
Profits, through production, 104
  through restriction, 104
Providence Journal, 116
Purchasing power, 103
Purdue University, 91–92

Q

Quality improvement, 48

R

Railway Mediation Act, 14
Ramond, Albert, 25
Rate cutting, 72
Reader's Digest, The, 112
Remington Arms, 46
Restrictionists, 104
Revere Copper, 46
Right to strike, 108
Roper, Elmo, 12
Ruml, Beardsley, 105
Ruttenberg, Harold, 11

S

St. Louis Post-Dispatch, 112
Scandanavia, 14
Scarcity philosophy, 24
Scarcity practices, 102
Scientific management, 26, 56, 73, 100
Second World War, 24
Self-government, 35
Senate Education and Labor Committee, 99
Single-rate wage payment, 85
Social responsibility, 122
  of labor, 122
  of management, 122
Society for the Advancement of Management, 63

Socony-Vacuum Company, 94
Speed rating, 61
Speed-up, 25
Sperry Gyroscope Company, 83–84
Stakhanovite movement, 98
Standards of living, 111
Statesmanship, business, 103–104
Stretch-out, 25
Suggestion-award system, 49–50

T

Tariffs, advocacy of high, 77
Taylor, Frederick W., 73
Time-and-motion study, 56
Time rates, 60
Time standards, 56
Time study, 16, 21, 56, 61–65, 67–68, 97, 99
Time-study stewards, 65, 67
Toledo Labor Management Citizens Committee, 111
Toledo Plan, 113–115, 118
Training Within Industry, 94–98
Turner, John, 13

U

Union growth, 120
Union participation in policy making, 65–66
Union regulation, 21
Unions, acceptance of, 6, 14, 50
    illegal, 14
    toleration of, 14
United Automobile Workers, 23, 74, 75, 99
U.S. Chamber of Commerce, 77, 106, 115–116
United States Steel, 46, 117
United Steelworkers, 117

Unity of effort, 72
University of Michigan, 29
University of Vermont, 56

V

Voluntary machinery for dispute settlement, 109

W

Wage determination, systematic, 80
Wage differentials, 107–108
Wage levels, 107–108
Wage policy, 87
    sound, 79–80, 86
Wage rules, 87–88
Wage scales, 107
Wage schedules, 87
Wage structure, 80, 83, 88
Wages, increased, 30
Wagner Act, 13, 89
War Labor Board, 70
War Production Board, 45, 97
Washington Post, 112
Waste elimination, 48
Western Electric, 94
Westinghouse Company, 48, 71
White, Leslie, 29
White Paper, "Employment Policy," 26
Wilson, C. E., 46
Wilson, Woodrow, 54
    Commission on the Causes of Industrial Unrest (1912) under, 13
Work measurement, 57–59, 61–68, 82
Work methods, 70
    best, 75
Worker efficiency, 61